Contents

Foreword

WHEN ROBERT BOLGER WAS at Claremont Graduate University in the middle of writing the dissertation on which this book is based, his mentor and dissertation advisor, the distinguished Wittgensteinian philosopher of religion, D. Z. Phillips, died unexpectedly. For reasons that will be apparent from the arguments of the introduction and chapter 4, he felt very uncomfortable about approaching the other major systematic theologian and philosopher of theology at Claremont, Phillip Clayton, to advise him. Somehow he was directed to me, and though I am neither a philosopher nor a theologian of any kind, both his project and his prose style appealed to me greatly.

Bolger's goal was and continues to be to offer a critique of what he calls *religious scientism*, which he sees as an attempt to gain credibility for religion by linking it to the methods, concepts, and attitudes of modern science, an enterprise that is highly valued, at least among academics and other self-professed intellectuals in our culture. This project interests me both because, as an historian I have a long-standing interest in *scientism* in general as well as in the historical interactions between religion and science.[1] Furthermore, I am very sympathetic to Bolger's core claim that the attempt to support religion using scientific arguments often involves major misunderstandings regarding the goals and language of religion or science as well as dangers that religious or scientific meanings will be unintentionally transformed in the process.

Secondly, although Bolger develops a series of sophisticated philosophical and theological arguments, he does so using language that is remarkably jargon free, and his prose is filled with clear and down to earth illustrations. Since one of my long-term goals has been to expand

---

1. Richard Olson, *Science and Scientism in 19th Century Europe.* Urbana-Champaign, IL: University of Illinois Press, 2009; also Richard Olson, *Science and Religion, 1450–1900: From Copernicus through Darwin.* Westport, CT: Greenwood, 2004.

the audience for religion and science relationships beyond that of professional and aspiring theologians and historians of science or religion, Bolger's clear and forceful style appeals greatly.

It has often been claimed, especially by those who are critics of traditional religion, that because both scientific and religious activities include propositions and involve the use of models, a central goal of each is to explain our *experiences*. That is surely what Aristotle was claiming when he argued that the Milesian *physicoi* offered a new way of accounting for events in the sixth century BCE than earlier *theologoi* had used.[2] It was undoubtedly what August Comte, the French founder of nineteenth-century positivism intended when he articulated his Law of Three Stages, according to which "each branch of our knowledge passes successively through three different theoretical conditions: the Theological, or fictitious; the Metaphysical, or abstract, and the Scientific, or positive."[3] And it is a view explicitly articulated by the contemporary arch-atheist, Richard Dawkins when he writes that, "the most basic claims of religion are scientific."[4]

Curiously, most of those who engage in religious scientism seem to accept very nearly the same claim when they implicitly accept the notion that religion and science are both aimed at generating knowledge and that in judging the merits of any knowledge claim one should appeal to criteria drawn from scientific activities. Yet as Bolger makes very clear, this basic set of claims involves a series of major misunderstandings that depend upon the fact that common terms have radically different meanings within religious communities of discourse and scientific communities of discourse.

One central misunderstanding is that the primary goal of religion is to produce knowledge of the kind that science seeks to produce. Neither individual religious propositions nor religious models function like scientific ones. While scientific propositions are intended to be about intersubjectively observable facts and must thus be subject to empirical testing, religious propositions generally express personal attitudes and values that are not, in principle, observable. Thus, for example, when

2. Aristotle, *Metaphysics*, 982b 11–27.

3. Auguste Comte, *The Positive Philosophy*. Translated by Harriet Martineau. Reprint. New York: AMS, 1974.

4. Richard Dawkins, "The Nullifidian," quoted in Mark Johnson, *Saving God*. Princeton: Princeton University Press, 2009, 46.

religious persons state that God made the world, they are not making a factual claim that can be checked like the claim that hydrogen and oxygen can combine to form water. They are stating that they view the world as a gift. Though Bolger does not use these terms, anthropologists accept the notion that almost all human communities embrace two radically different and complementary ways of relating to the world. One of these they characterize as "causal"—an "I-it" relationship that includes the kind of distancing and affective neutrality that science seeks to achieve. The other they characterize as "participatory"—an "I-thou" relationship that involves an existential immediacy and shared affects.[5] With rare exceptions, religious terminology reflects participatory relationships. While one or another of these orientations may dominate in a community, both are, and I suspect, to some extent must be present. As David Sloan Wilson argues,

> Once [scientific] reasoning is removed from its pedestal as the only adaptive way to think, a host of alternatives become available. Emotions are evolved mechanisms for motivating adaptive behavior that are far more ancient than the cognitive processes typically associated with scientific thought. . . . [W]e might expect stories, music, and rituals to be at least as important as logical arguments in orchestrating the behavior of groups. Supernatural agents and events . . . can provide blueprints for action that far surpass factual accounts of the natural world in clarity and motivating power.[6]

Just as propositions in religion do not function as knowledge claims about objective facts, Bolger argues compellingly that religious models do not function as representations of facts but rather as attitude and activity orienting entities supported by religious rituals.

In each of the central chapters of this book Bolger analyses in detail the misunderstandings involved in one of the major claims made by those who he identifies as key players in contemporary religious scientism. After defining the varieties of religious scientism and dealing with the confusion over the use of models for different purposes, he focuses in chapter 2 on Ian Barbour's importation of critical realism into theology from philosophy of science and the misunderstandings it creates when

5. See, for example, Stanley Tambiah, *Magic, Science, and the Scope of Rationality.* Cambridge: Cambridge University Press, 1990, 105–7.

6. David Sloan Wilson, *Darwin's Cathedral: Evolution, Religion, and the Nature of Society.* Chicago: University of Chicago Press, 2002, 41–42.

applied to notions like God, which are in principle unobservable. In chapter 3 he explores the misunderstanding of the nature of scientific explanation involved in William Dembski's attempt to create a science of Intelligent Design. In chapter 4 he analyzes misunderstandings regarding the notions of closed causal chains and downward causality in Philip Clayton's attempt to use the cognitive sciences and notions of mental causation to make divine action plausible without suspending causality in the physical world. And in chapter 5 he discusses Arthur Peacocke's defense of "Panentheism"—i.e., the doctrine that the universe is in God but that God is more than the physical universe—in theological cosmology and explores the confusions between what we mean when we say that we live "in" God, where "in" has neither spatial nor temporal meaning, and what the physical scientist means when she says that the milk was *in* the refrigerator yesterday.

Finally, Bolger concludes with a chapter on how science and religion can co-exist as equally valued but largely independent orientations in our lives. If along the way we are treated to the wit and wisdom of Mark Twain, Simone Weil, Lewis Carrol, Grimm's Fairy Tales, Leo Tolstoy, and many other literary giants. How could one possibly lose!

Richard Olson
Professor of History and Willard W. Keith Jr. Fellow in Humanities
Harvey Mudd College, Claremont California

Acknowledgments

I WOULD LIKE TO thank Robert Coburn for his friendship, companionship, and ability to always appear interested no matter what topic I ramble on about. I also wish to thank the late D. Z. Phillips and the late David Foster Wallace without whose encouragement and support this work would have never been possible. I wish to thank Patrick Horn and Genevieve Beenen for their wonderful and thorough editing skills. I am also grateful to Richard Olson, Brian Keeley, and Patrick Horn for reading various drafts of this book as it progressed through its many transformations. Mostly, I want to thank my wife Lara, my dog Annie, and my sister Maureen for filling my life with Love, wonder, and inspiration.

INTRODUCTION

Fighting for a Place at the Trough

I N HIS ESSAY "SCIENCE and Solidarity," Richard Rorty writes that "any academic discipline which wants a place at the trough, but is unable to offer the predictions and the technology provided by the natural sciences, must either pretend to imitate science or find some way of obtaining 'cognitive' status without the necessity of discovering facts."[1] Since precious little of what we usually count as academically significant work ever makes an impact on popular opinion, Rorty's remark likely reveals that the influence has moved in the other direction. That is, it seems more likely that the man-in-the-street's love for all things scientific has become a codified creedal statement forming part of the core of what we think of as rigorous academic work (it may be that C. P. Snow's "Two Cultures" are alive and well[2]). I would guess that at least part of our current fascination with science is best accounted for by the incredible amount of technological success that we have enjoyed. This success in the natural sciences has indeed aided our day-to-day existence in innumerable ways. Yet, behind the banal praise of the technological triumphs that have made our lives (on the average) longer and (for the most part) easier, there is, I think, the more deeply philosophical feeling that the natural sciences are getting it right. That is, technological success appears to offer some proof that the description of reality given by the natural sciences is correct, and, in some ways this kind of thinking appears justified. You cannot cure diseases if the germ theory is utterly false and a rocket ship will not arrive at its destination if your physics is simply a fictitious description of the natural world. As C. S. Peirce writes, "[A] man [or woman] must be downright

1. Rorty, *Objectivity*, 35.
2. See Snow, *The Two Cultures*.

1

crazy to deny that science has made many true discoveries."[3] The problem, however, is not with being in awe of, infatuated with, or inspired by science. The problem is not even in thinking that science has revealed to us some incredibly true things about the world we live in. The problem, at least as far as I can tell, is that with the success of science (technologically, or in its description of the natural world) there comes the tendency to reify the practice of science into the best, or only, way to discover truths about reality. This, in turn, leads to the type of academic fondness for science mentioned by Rorty, but worse, it leads to other disciplines trying to *appear* scientific as a way of fighting for their place at the trough of academic acceptance. This sort of intellectual mimicry led Wittgenstein to write, "Philosophers constantly see the method of science before their eyes, and are irresistibly tempted to ask and answer questions in the way science does."[4] We can now safely say that this tendency (for good or for ill) extends far beyond the work of the philosopher.

The goal of this book is to look at how the tendency to imitate science has affected the contemporary study of the relationship between science and religion. Specifically, I want to see how a particular desire to make religion look more scientific by merging religious belief with the methods and concepts of science has created certain, very specific, conceptual confusions. Of course, wanting to make religion look scientific is a direct result of the desire to avoid academic alienation. If Rorty was correct, and I think he was, and if academic disciplines must either become a science or (at least) look like one, then it would appear to behoove the theologian to attempt to make religion look more like a science. There is thus a prevalent feeling that science has thrown down the gauntlet that theology must now pick up if it is not going to be laughed out of town. Arthur Peacocke and Philip Clayton seem to be acutely aware of the intellectual challenge that is facing religion in the contemporary "age of science." Clayton writes that many academics "now question whether intellectuals should engage theology at all, at least with anything more than archeological interest."[5] Peacocke adds, "The credibility of all religions is at stake under the impact of: new understandings of the natural world, of the place of humanity in it and of the very nature of personhood; and—even more corrosively—the

3. Peirce, *The Essential Peirce*, 217.
4. Wittgenstein, *The Blue and the Brown Books*, 18.
5. Clayton, *Adventures*, 24.

loss of respect for the intellectual integrity of religious thinking in general and of Christian theology in particular."[6] In this case, if religious belief (or theological inquiry) is going to retain (or regain) a seat at the academic trough, it must engage (in some substantive way) with the truth claims of modern science. Clayton writes, "Many of us believe that the growing field of religion-science has helped to relegitimate religion 'for an age of science.'"[7] However, the question remains as to how this "religitimation" process is supposed to take place, and whether its occurrence is even philosophically viable.

LISTENING TO DAWKINS

One way to begin to see how certain Christian theologians have sought to reinstate the academic reliability of religion is to look backwards from the arguments of one of religion's most infamous modern critics, Richard Dawkins. In a sense, Dawkins's anti-religious crusade can be seen as an attempt to fight for the legitimacy of science in the face of what he thinks are competing truth claims about the nature of reality; the putative truth claims offered up by religious believers. One of Dawkins's strategies (though not the only one) is to show the superiority of scientific explanations over religious ones by showing how the truth of scientific explanations falsify religious claims made about the nature of reality. Of course, for this argument to even make sense, religious beliefs must be operating within the same logical category as their scientific counterparts, otherwise, there would be no way to adequately compare the two sets of claims about the world, and hence no possibility of falsification. This is no problem for Dawkins, however, since he takes religious beliefs to be scientific claims about the nature of reality. He writes, "The Virgin Birth, the Resurrection, the Raising of Lazarus, the manifestations of Mary and the Saints around the Catholic world, even the Old Testament miracles, all are freely used for religious propaganda, . . . Every one of these miracles amounts to a scientific claim, a violation of the normal running of the natural world."[8] Similarly he writes, "You can't escape the scientific implications of religion. A universe with a God would look quite different from a universe without one. A physics, a biology where there is a God is bound to look

6. Peacocke, *Paths From Science*, 15.

7. Clayton, *Adventures*, 52.

8. Richard Dawkins, *A Devil's Chaplain*, 150.

different. So the most basic claims of religion are scientific. Religion is a scientific theory."[9] While there are innumerable problems with these statements (including spelling out the differences between a world with God and a world without God), the main point is that Dawkins claims that religion represents a sort of scientific theory (or set of theories).

Now, of course, once the argument against religion is set up this way, Dawkins indeed has a fairly straightforward way to proceed. If religious beliefs are seen as scientific hypotheses (or explanations) in competition with the claims made in science, then we can use various scientific tools and presuppositions to see who is offering the best hypothesis (or explanation). This method would be no different from the way that scientists generally decide on the explanatory efficacy of two competing hypothetical explanations. In the end they would amass evidence, advance experiments, and attempt to falsify certain claims. They would then hold a conference to discuss their findings, unveiling, on the final day, the explanatory winner. The problem is that it appears something has gone amiss here. Is religion actually a scientific theory that can compete with science on scientific terms? Even worse, if science is being extended to eliminate religious beliefs that really are not scientific (or even pseudo-scientific) at all, then Dawkins is simply extending science into a domain where it does not belong. In this case he has left his profession of science far behind.

Some have seen through Dawkins's argument and questioned its validity claiming that Dawkins both misconstrues religious belief and overextends scientific inquiry. This is what prompts Karl Giberson to write of Dawkins that "there is no escaping it. Dawkins is a good scientist and a brilliant communicator . . . but he seems strangely unaware that he is an abysmal philosopher and an even worse theologian."[10] It is also why Mark Johnston claims that the arguments of Dawkins (and his *New Atheists* colleagues) are appealing only to those "who mange to combine spiritual tone deafness with a naïve view of scientific method."[11] Yet as bad as Dawkins's arguments tend to be, the question remains: what makes him think that this is the way to respond to religion in the first place?

---

9. Dawkins, "The Nullifidian." Quoted in Johnston, *Saving God*, 46.

10. Giberson, *Oracles of Science*, 40.

11. Johnston, *Saving God,* 38.

The interesting question to me is thus not whether Dawkins-type arguments are effective, but why one would desire to argue in the way that he does. If philosophers and theologians desire, as indeed Mark Johnston does in his book, *Saving God*, to show that religion is not a science, what would motivate Dawkins to argue against religious beliefs as if they were scientific claims? Unfortunately, Dawkins is not alone in thinking of religion as a sort of intellectual competitor vying with science for the minds of individuals; rather, he is prodded and goaded on by certain scholars writing today in the area of science and religion (the area that we would expect Dawkins to be quite familiar with). The problem is not only that Dawkins is paying too little attention to philosophy of religion and theology, but rather that he is paying too much attention to the contemporary work of science and religion.

Rather than spending time describing conceptual differences between scientific and religious concepts, many scholars writing in science and religion find it profitable to both explain a neutral way of talking about rationality that applies equally to both science and religion, and to find ways of using the methods and concepts of science as a means of making religion look more scientifically acceptable. The former is a way of arguing that science does not have a monopoly on truth and rationality while the latter is a way of showing that religion may look more like a science than some have thought. If all instances of truth (with a small "t") are actually an attempt to get at the Truth (with a big "T"), then we might expect that some of the concepts of science and religion could (to some extent) be, *mutatis mutandis*, interchangeable. But this requires that there be certain univocal concepts (such as truth, rationality, explanation) in place that can be used across contexts to judge the efficacy of truth claims in science and religion without being specific to either discipline. In the chapters to come I want to look specifically at how attempts to interchangeably mix certain aspects of science and religion can create more problems than solutions. However, for the remainder of this introduction I will make the philosophical argument that the attempt to find a univocal way of judging truth claims in science and religion can never even get off the ground.

RATIONALITY FULL STOP

There are times when Philip Clayton writes as if the meaning of "rationality" is multifarious and context dependent, such as when he writes, "No definitive list of standards sufficient for rationality will be provided, since the nature of the discourse and the context of the discussion play an essential role in what counts as rational."[12] Or, when he states that, "thinkers like Wittgenstein, Habermas, and Foucault have shown, there is an irresistible plurality of rationalities corresponding to the different goals and contexts of human action."[13] But what Clayton offers with his right hand he takes away with his left when he writes, "if the use of the term *rational* is not to be merely equivocal, it appears necessary that there be at least some commonalities between the diverse disciplines that claim to offer rational explanations."[14] But what makes it necessary for all coherent uses of "rational" to have some common ground? What if, upon investigation, we actually do find various uses of rationality? Clayton allows for this possibility, but circumvents the possibility of conceptual relativity by stipulating that while there may indeed be many different contextual uses of rationality, there must still be a univocal way to justify these various uses. The discussion is simply shifted from rationality *per se* to the rational assessment of rationality.

Clayton's strategy is simple, he makes it a necessary condition of knowledge claims that these claims be able to be discussed, criticized, and rationally justified across disciplines. He presents this condition as the *intersubjective principle*, which he defines as "the principle that only those assertions should count as knowledge that are able to win support within existing discussions in and between the academic disciplines."[15] Of course, if a necessary condition of knowledge is going to be its ability to be criticized, discussed and justified across disciplines, what we still need are a set of rational principles that can serve as criteria for judging various knowledge claims when they occur; criteria that are not themselves context dependent. That is, there must be principles of rational justification general enough to float across all disciplines in order to be able to judge when a rational explanation has occurred (or true knowledge has

---

12. Clayton, *Explanations*, 6.

13. Ibid., 8.

14. Ibid. Emphasis in original.

15. Clayton, *Adventures in the Spirit*, 28.

been obtained) in either science or religion (or, for that matter, any other discipline), since if these principles were derived from any one discipline, we would simply have a case of imposing one discipline's use of rationality on another. Therefore, Clayton states that in order to explain the meaning of religious (or, in his case, Christian) truth claims to the wider intellectual community, the theologian will have to rely on "categories not drawn from the Christian tradition, as well as the use of *general* notions such as truth, meaning, and reference . . ."[16] But that is not all. In order to judge the intersubjective efficacy of a rational explanation, Clayton also relies on a general set of necessary conditions: external reference, truth, validity, and rationality. If a claim to rational explanation can meet these criteria, then that claim can be intersubjectively defended and the claim to knowledge can be justified.

The importance of Clayton's commitment to the *intersubjective principle* and to his claim to be in possession of certain "general notions" and "necessary conditions" is that these allow him to circumvent the simple pushing aside of religious claims to rationality. There will, of course, be a certain amount of discussion necessary between disciplines in order to decide whether one has offered a rational explanation or not, but given that we have in hand a set of "general notions" and "necessary conditions" the discussion can occur in a forum open to all disciplines. This creates a neutral playing field whereby explanations in science and religion can be justified or rejected. It also allows religion to compete with science as one academic discipline vying with another in order to justify its truth claims using the same neutral rational principles.

Employing a methodological approach that is similar to Clayton's, Arthur Peacocke seeks to justify the rationality of religious explanations by appealing to C. S. Peirce's scientific use of abductive reasoning (or what is often called an "inference to the best explanation"). Abduction is primarily a way of talking about how scientific inferences (or hypotheses) are formulated. Peirce writes, "All the ideas of science come to it by the way of Abduction. Abduction consists in studying facts and devising a theory to explain them."[17] An abductive inference begins with a certain state of affairs we are seeking to explain, and then seeks to offer a set of sufficient conditions that purports to adequately explain the phenomenon

16. Clayton, *Explanations*, 161.

17. Peirce, *The Essential Peirce*, 205.

in question. While Peirce primarily thought of abduction as a tool for scientific inquiry, Peacocke thinks that due to the fact that our reasoning processes in general are the product of biological evolution, we are well suited to offer explanations for events in various contexts whether in the natural sciences or in the humanities (including theology). These various explanations, according to Peacocke, all take the form of an "inference to the best explanation," which Peacocke describes as a form of reasoning in which "we infer what would, if true, provide the best of competing explanations of the data we can generate."[18] In a sense an explanation is simply a posited answer (even a guess) used to explain a specific "why question" (for example, "Why is x this way rather than that?"). Peacocke thinks that the type of explanations offered by an inference to the best explanation are not strictly falsifiable (although it is not clear why he thinks this). Thus he writes, "Hence it is particularly apt for theology to adopt this IBE [inference to the best explanation] model, which is so adequate for science and everyday life, since overt falsifying of theological affirmations is notoriously unavailable."[19]

If Peacocke's use of inference to the best explanation is going to be able to do the interdisciplinary work that he requires of it, then, much like Clayton, he is going to need a set of context-neutral conditions that can be used in order to judge when an explanation is actually the "best" of the lot. Luckily (for us or for him), he has a set of conditions ready-at-hand. Peacocke offers the following five criteria as a means of judging whether an explanation is indeed the "best explanation": comprehensiveness, fruitfulness, general cogency and plausibility, internal coherence and consistency, simplicity or elegance. If an explanation can meet these criteria better than its competitors, we may infer (admitting the possibility of being wrong) that we have obtained something like the best explanation. Since Peacocke's criteria are supposed to be general enough to decide between competing hypotheses offered across disciplines, what he offers is a way for competing hypotheses to be judged intersubjectively by individuals in different disciplines. He approvingly quotes Clayton and Knapp when they write, "The task of rational discussion is to weigh competing explanations, whatever their respective sources, and to select the one or more that do the best job of explaining the data at hand . . .

18. Peacocke, *Paths from Science*, 27.

19. Ibid.

Accomplishing this task involves making religious beliefs available to intersubjective assessment . . ."[20] By utilizing general principles, Peacocke, not unlike Clayton, has offered a way to level the playing field amongst various explanations in various disciplines allowing theological explanations to compete "fairly" amongst their scientific kin.

What Clayton and Peacocke have accomplished is two-fold. First, they have attempted to take Rorty seriously by trying to show how religion *can* compete for rational assent with science by showing that religious knowledge is more like scientific knowledge than we may have thought. Second, they have paved the way for arguments like those offered by Dawkins to make a certain amount of sense. Now the question is this: What sense do their own arguments make?

CONCEPTS WITHOUT A HOME

Much of the career of the philosopher D. Z. Phillips was plagued with individuals criticizing him for relegating the existence of God to a mere word in a language-game; a word that had no *real* external referent. This criticism persisted throughout his career despite the fact that Phillips, just as persistently, tried to clarify his position. In one of his final books he writes, "Am I saying that believers are only answerable to their words? Obviously not. They are answerable to God."[21] The problem wasn't that Phillips was ambiguous about whether God's existence amounted to the simple existence of a word, rather, he was interested in what words such as "real," "exist," and "reference" mean when they were used in a religious context. Phillips writes, "There is a conception of an independent reality in religion. Yet, to see what this conception of an independent reality amounts to, we must pay attention to the grammar of the religious concepts involved."[22] For Phillips, paying attention to grammar is simply paying attention to how a word functions in its standard use. It does no good to talk about the independent reality of God without saying what "independent" and "reality" mean *in a religious context*. Often philosophers simply italicize the words *exist* and *real* as a way of attempting to show that they have the most robust meaning of these terms in mind

20. Clayton and Knapp, "Rationality and Christian Self-Conceptions," 134. Quoted in Peacocke, *Paths from Science*, 29.

21. Phillips, *The Problem of Evil*, 169.

22. Phillips, *Wittgenstein*, 25.

when they apply them to God. But, as Phillips responds, "nothing is achieved by italicizing these words. The task of clarifying their grammar when they are used remains."[23] Phillips's work was partly presented as a way of persistently turning philosophers' minds back towards the actual way that religious concepts are *used* rather than imposing on them meanings that were foreign to the religious life and practice.

The concern with the relationship between context and meaning is not simply one that is required of religious concepts, it is also a necessity when it comes to looking at the way that religious concepts are related to concepts used in other disciplines, including the disciplines of science. Phillips writes, "To ask after the meaning of a concept in ordinary discourse is to ask for its meaning in the normal context of its usage. If the concept in question is scientific or religious, the context of ordinary discourse will be scientific or religious, respectively."[24] In this case, attempting to relate science and religion would be preceded by an investigation into how words such as "truth," "existence," "meaning," "explanation," "justification," "knowledge," etc. function in each discipline. This would rule out the possibility of applying an *a priori* stipulative definition to such concepts in order to show how various disciplines must dialogue if there is going to be rational discourse.

In *Philosophical Investigations*, Wittgenstein writes "They *must* have something in common, or they would not be called 'games'—but *look and see* whether there is anything common to all. . . . To repeat: don't think, but look!"[25] It should now be obvious where Clayton and Peacocke have gone astray. In attempting to find some sort of conceptual "neutral ground" whereby religion and science can be related they have sacrificed the hard work of paying attention to the meaning of concepts in the specific contexts in which they are used. They have thought too much and looked too little. It does no good to simply say that you are delineating the meaning of a set of concepts that are free of any contextual constraints without attempting to show how these concepts have purchase in the contexts under question. For example, when Clayton decides that in order for a knowledge claim to be justified it must be intersubjectively discussed and criticized, in what context is he using such an account of knowledge?

23. Ibid., 35.
24. Phillips, *The Problem of Evil*, 6.
25. Wittgenstein, *Philosophical Investigations*, § 66.

Furthermore, when he stipulates that the necessary conditions of an inter-subjective rational explanation are external reference, truth, validity, and rationality, in what context is he spelling out the meaning of these terms? Are all claims to knowledge sufficiently similar that such context-neutral principles are adequate? When Job said, "I know that my redeemer lives" (Job 19:25), was he making a claim with the same logical structure as "I know that my wife loves me," "I know that relativity is true," "I know that I have five dollars in my pocket," or, "I know that this is a hand"? Of course, the only way to answer this question is to first determine the meaning of each statement, which then necessarily requires looking at the context in which each is spoken. The same question applies to Clayton's necessary conditions themselves. Is Job's reference to a redeemer an "external reference" that is of the same logical structure as the "external reference" a teacher makes when she holds up her hand and says to a small child, "*Hand*"? It would appear that Job's "redeemer" has a vastly different type of reality than a hand. In each case, in order to figure out what external reference means we have to look at the meaning of the words in their context of use. We cannot, *pace* Clayton, simply act as if there are aspects of language that simply *must* have a univocal meaning across all contexts simply because of our penchant for intersubjective dialogue.

We see something similar going on when Peacocke speaks of context-free principles that can help us decide if an explanation is the best one or not. It would seem that the meaning of Peacocke's criteria of comprehensiveness, fruitfulness, general cogency and plausibility, internal coherence and consistency, and simplicity or elegance, are going to vary depending on whether we are speaking about an explanation for a scientific hypothesis or the claim that the world is a place where God dwells. Take the criterion of "simplicity," for example. We can imagine what it would be for one scientific theory to be simpler than another competing theory; say one theory posits less unobservable entities. But what if a scientific theory is competing with a theological explanation? Is there a univocal sense of "simplicity" that can be used in such a case? It may be that since God is supposedly a metaphysical simple, God always wins the simplicity debate by default. But this is not because God is a more simple explanation, but because simplicity has a different meaning in the context of God-talk than in the context of scientific theories. What about the criterion of "explanatory comprehensiveness"? We can imagine a theory that fails to account for some state of affairs and another competing theory that can satisfactorily explain that particular phenomenon. But can a scientific theory compete with an explanatory theory that is not even in principle falsifiable (as many theological claims are not). Does this type of explanation again win by default? Finally, how about the criterion of plausibility? Does Peacocke mean plausible to Alvin Plantinga or plausible to Steven Weinberg? Both seem to be rational individuals, yet they have vastly different explanations for the origin of the cosmos. In fact, they may have basic differences on what they count as plausible explanations, and these differences may just be the *result* of their explanations rather than a way to decide which explanation is correct.

In the case of Clayton and Peacocke, the methodological flaw is the same. The problem is that their supposedly neutral concepts, which are developed to allow religion to rejoin the academic debate on rationality, are either contextually homeless (and, hence meaningless), or they are taken from the natural sciences and applied to claims made in religion. As I stated, it does no good to simply demand that there *must* be a univocal use of these concepts as if the converse was somehow logically impossible. D. Z. Phillips aptly summarizes what I take to be the main criticism against Clayton and Peacocke when he writes, "One can say within any such context, whether it be science or religion, 'This is the rule which must be observed, this is the meaning which a word must have if it is to belong to this conceptual family.' But when philosophers say, 'This is the meaning which a word must have' without specifying any context, they are guilty of arbitrary linguistic legislation. The 'must' is not a logical 'must,' but simply the 'must' of their own preferences, or the 'must' of one context which they have elevated, consciously or unconsciously, to be a standard for all others."[26]

LAYING THE FOUNDATION FOR A RELIGIOUS SCIENTISM

While Peacocke and Clayton have not given us an adequate way to relate science and religion, they have given us a way to recognize what has gone wrong in the contemporary science/religion discussion. In a sense, their methodological flaws represent the heart of what I call "religious scientism." It does little good, however, to simply state that a philosophical error has been made without attempting to show, through various examples, what exactly has gone wrong. As D. Z. Phillips writes, "It is

26. Phillips, *Faith and Philosophical*, 63–64.

not a matter of anyone *saying* that there are differences between modes of discourse, but *looking* to see whether there are, and if there are, *showing* their character."[27] Most of what has been written thus far is simply a form of stage-setting, a prolegomena for the specific examples of religious scientism that follow. However, before looking at these examples, it is necessary to formulate, as clearly as possible, just what is meant by *religious scientism*, showing how this concept differs from (and is related to) scientism as it is more generally used.

27. Ibid., 64. Emphasis in the original.

1

Religious Scientism
and Its Secular Counterparts

O BTAINING CLARITY ABOUT THE meaning of a philosophical concept such as scientism need not always involve fancy philosophical musings or tedious distinctions between different uses of language. Sometimes simple humor does the trick, as in Mark Twain's *Life on the Mississippi*:

> In the space of one hundred and seventy-six years the Lower Mississippi has shortened itself two hundred and forty-two miles. That is an average of a trifle over one mile and a third per year. Therefore, any calm person, who is not blind or idiotic, can see that in the Old Oolitic Silurian Period, just a million years ago next November, the Lower Mississippi River was upwards of one million three hundred thousand miles long, and stuck out over the Gulf of Mexico like a fishing-rod. And by the same token any person can see that seven hundred and forty-two years from now the Lower Mississippi will be only a mile and three-quarters long, and Cairo and New Orleans will have joined their streets together, and be plodding comfortably along under a single mayor and a mutual board of aldermen. There is something fascinating about science. One gets such wholesale returns of conjecture out of such a trifling investment of fact.[1]

Twain's humor is used here to make two related but different points. First, scientific facts can be stretched and distorted in all sorts of silly ways, and second, the silliness can be camouflaged if it is presented with a certain amount of pomposity and scientific hubris. The lesson seems to be that if you can quote scientific facts with enough seriousness, there

---

1. Twain, *Life on the Mississippi*, 136.

will always be some seemingly serious people who will take what you say seriously no matter how far fetched your conjectures.

This, in a nutshell, is scientism. In its broadest sense, scientism can be seen as a misuse (or misapplication) of the facts and/or methods of science. Of course, the difference between Twain's account and those who really practice scientism is that Twain was being funny. Most individuals who seek to apply something like science with a broad brush are usually not humorists but serious scientists and scientific popularizers who are trying (however misguided their efforts) to make sense of the world in which they live. In attempting to make sense of scientism on the way to presenting the view I call religious scientism, I want to take Twain's humor seriously. That is, I want to attempt to see how it is that science gets distorted in the practice of scientism while also attempting to make sense of the straight-faced delivery with which scientism is presented. I think that part of the problem is that we do not generally feel the intuitive lure of scientism as we seek to criticize it and declare it silly. However, lest we think that scientism is simply the naïve mistake of those with a romantic longing for the heady days of logical positivism, or the result of a certain arrogant pomposity by the scientifically sophisticated (albeit the philosophically naïve), it is profitable to look at some of the legitimate reasons why people (especially scientifically-minded people) are attracted to scientism in the first place. We can do this best if we can get a foothold on some of the goals that accompany the practice of science in its numerous manifestations.

SCIENTISM AND THE GOALS OF SCIENCE

In her paper "Six Signs of Scientism," Susan Haack offers a practical guide for recognizing when someone has slipped from the legitimate practice of science to the more philosophically problematic practice of scientism. For our purposes here, I am interested in two of Haack's six signs (although the other four certainly have their purpose); namely, I am interested in the claim that some individuals practicing scientism tend to adopt "the manners, the trappings, the technical terminology, etc., of the sciences, irrespective of their real usefulness,"[2] and, the tendency of scientism to look "to the sciences for answers to questions beyond their scope."[3]

2. Haack, "Six Signs." Forthcoming in Haack, *Putting Philosophy to Work*.
3. Ibid.

Both of these signs, much like Mark Twain's example, are indicative of scientism's tendency to extend the concepts and/or methods of science beyond their standard context, irrespective of whether or not the new application actually produces anything like scientific results. Of course, spotting these signs in practice is a bit trickier than one may think. This is mainly because the practice of scientism tends to be shrouded by the legitimate goals of the sciences. Such goals function fine in the context of a particular scientific project, but tend to lose their explanatory power (and often their meaning as well) when applied too broadly. Part of understanding scientism, in both its standard presentation and in its contemporary religious use, is to understand just what these goals are and how they get distorted.

Since there is no single entity called "science" (anymore than there is a single entity called "reality"), it would be hard to delineate a single goal of science. This is why I often refer to "science" as "the sciences." That being said, we can identify general *goals* that apply across the scientific disciplines and that loosely form a set of aspirations that scientists seek to abide by in one form or another. For instance, we may safely say that the following represent a general account of the goals of the sciences even though the specific applications of these goals may differ slightly from discipline to discipline and from context to context.

1. *Ontological goal:* Within the practices of the science, scientists seek to delineate the true (or real) from the fictitious (or unreal).

2. *Epistemological goal:* Within the practices of the science, scientists seek to delineate true instances of knowledge from instances of *mere* belief (or conjecture).

3. *Explanatory goal:* Within the practices of the science, scientists seek to clarify and explain (or make more precise) some of the concepts used in other (traditionally non-scientific) disciplines.

Of course, since *reality, knowledge,* and *explanatory success* all have a variety of specific applications depending on which branch of science we are talking about, the actual details of each concept's use may vary slightly from discipline to discipline. That being said, however, these variegated uses will tend to share certain family resemblances.

The distortion of these goals (either singly or jointly) occur due to what I call "context switching." Context switching happens when a word from one context is used in another while trying to retain the meaning of the word in its first context. That is, one takes a word that has a meaning in a specific context and attempts to give it the same meaning in a different context (or, worse yet, across all contexts where the word is used). We saw specific examples of "context-switching" in the introduction when it was shown how Philip Clayton attempted to define "rationality" in a univocal way across various contexts and how Arthur Peacocke sought to do something similar with the concept "explanation." As I mentioned in the introduction, this type of context switching creates problems by forcing words and meanings into foreign contexts. Of course, the solution to this problem is to pay attention to the meanings that words actually have in the contexts in which they are used, but that is a lesson for a bit later. My main concern here is to show what happens when the goals of the sciences are taken from their scientific context and applied more broadly, distorting their original meanings. By demonstrating the conceptual errors that underlie scientism we will be able to accomplish two things on our way to defining religious scientism. First, we will be able to clearly see the kind of philosophical error that gives rise to scientism and, second, we will be able to understand why scientism appears to make intuitive sense while resulting in patent nonsense.

My claim is that when these types of conceptual and contextual distortions occur there will always be telltale signs that the goals of the sciences have been hijacked for a different purpose. These signs are what I have referred to (and will continue to refer to) as "conceptual confusions." That is, when the goals of the sciences (or concepts in general) get misused, the by-product will be a certain semantic breakdown. This is evident in Mark Twain's intentional misapplication of a true explanatory fact of science. In this case we can say that context switching is the cause of our problem while conceptual confusion is the effect. Of course, all of this does not mean that there is simply one entity called "scientism." Rather, as each goal of the sciences gets distorted in different ways, the result is different types (or senses) of scientism.

ONTOLOGICAL SCIENTISM

I stated above that the ontological goal of the sciences is simply the claim that within the various practices of science, scientists seek to delineate the true (or real) from the fictitious (or unreal). To state that one of the goals of science is to investigate reality is a bit of a truism; that is, it seems that investigating reality is part and parcel of what we mean by the practice of science (in its various instantiations). In fact, a science that did not list a desire to "discover what is real" as part of its mission statement would be an odd duck indeed. This should not be taken to mean that there are not serious disputes within science about what is real and what is not (the realism/antirealism debate is alive and well), but rather to say that these internal disputes do not diminish, but rather reinforce, the fact that science is intimately concerned with ontology. This is why the following definition of scientism, offered by Jerry Fodor, is at best incomplete and at worse misguided. Fodor writes, "I hold to the philosophical view that, for want of a better term, I'll call by one that is usually taken to be pejorative: *Scientism.* Scientism claims, on the one hand, that the goals of scientific inquiry include the discovery of objective empirical truths; on the other hand, that science has come pretty close to achieving this goal at least from time to time. . . . I'm inclined to think that Scientism, so construed, is not just true but *obviously and certainly* true . . ."[4] I agree with Fodor's definition as a general definition of science, and so, it seems to me, would most everybody else. In fact, it is hard to see how Fodor's scientism is anything more than a straightforward definition of the ontological goal of the sciences combined with a nod to some historical successes. But the definition is missing a crucial feature of scientism. What Fodor needs in order to move from an expression of the ontological goal of the sciences to a philosophically interesting version of scientism is the claim that not only do the sciences investigate the real, but the real simply *is* what the sciences investigate. The former claim concerns science and its various disciplines while the latter is a philosophical account of reality that excludes from reality whatever is not investigated by the sciences. Since, however, there is no straightforward path from the ontological goal of the sciences to this claim about the nature of *all* reality, we need to look a bit further into what ontological scientism claims.

As mentioned above, the goals of the sciences are all part and parcel of the specific practices of the sciences. However, any claim about the nature of reality *an sich* is a metaphysical claim that extends far beyond the reach of any particular branch of the sciences. In this case, what is needed to get from the ontological goal to a claim about the nature of reality is a

---

4. Fodor, "Is Science Biologically Possible?" 30.

metaphysical claim such as the following definition of naturalism offered by David Armstrong:

> *Naturalism* (N): "reality consists of nothing but a single all-embracing spatio-temporal system."[5]

Now if we add (N) to the ontological goal we can see how the ontological goal gets extended and twisted into an all-embracing claim about reality. This account is what I refer to as ontological scientism, which can be defined as follows:

> *Ontological scientism*: The belief that what is real consists solely of the spatio-temporal world that is revealed (or counterfactually reveal-able) by the natural sciences.

To see ontological scientism in action, we need look no further than Richard Dawkins. Dawkins offers up a clear example of ontological scientism when he writes that "[t]he real world, properly understood in the scientific way, is deeply beautiful and unfailingly interesting."[6] Even though ontological scientism is often presented as if it is the common sense view of reality that follows from science, it clearly has little to do with the particulars of scientific work and more to do with a metaphysical commitment to something like Armstrong's naturalism. In his book *Infinite Life*, Robert Thurman exposes the mythological aspect of the claim that ontological scientism follows naturally from the practice of science:

> Most of us with a modern education have been conditioned from an early age to accept a philosophically materialistic, so-called "scientific" worldview. This view of reality is not presented to us as a possible theory about the nature of life. Rather, it is presented dogmatically, as if it were a fact, the only thing, the one true reality. We are made to feel as if scientific geniuses had directly and comprehensively encountered this nihilistic worldview and verified it with mathematical precision using machines that produce "hard" data.[7]

This, of course, is not so (which is Thurman's point). Ontological scientism cannot be confirmed (or even logically defended) by anything like the sciences. It is best understood as a twisted and distorted version of the

5. Armstrong, "Naturalism," 261.

6. Dawkins, *A Devil's Chaplain*, 43.

7. Thurman, *Infinite Life*, 12.

ontological goal of the sciences, the original meaning of which becomes lost. Ontological scientism creates a metaphysical worldview out of a definitional truism, moving from the fairly humble claim that science investigates reality to the claim that all that exists is what science investigates.

EPISTEMOLOGICAL SCIENTISM

Of course, it isn't only the ontological goal that is susceptible to this type of distortion; the epistemological goal of the sciences is open to similar misuse. As defined earlier, the epistemological goal, broadly speaking, has to do with the desire of the sciences to separate instances of knowledge from instances of belief (or conjecture). This goal actually contains two quite different, though related, assumptions. First, it assumes that within each sub-discipline of the sciences there are some agreed upon propositions that are taken as paradigmatic cases of knowledge. These are not simple trivial facts such as "there is a world" or "matter exists" since these are not discipline specific; rather, these knowledge claims are ones accepted by the majority of those working in their respective sub-disciplines. These may include things like natural selection in biology, Boyle's law in chemistry, and general and special relativity in physics. These are all examples of discipline-specific cases of knowledge that are now readily accepted by individuals both inside and outside of the respective disciplines. But they are also knowledge claims that have been originally generated by the discipline in question and that now serve as foundational (though fallible) instances of knowledge within each specified discipline. To call these "foundational" simply means that those within the discipline that reject such claims to knowledge would find themselves on the outside of the discipline looking in. Second, the epistemological goal also assumes that within each sub-discipline of science there are certain procedures in place that are generally taken to be sufficiently reliable for the production of something that can suitably be called "knowledge." That is, a set of conditions (maybe experimental, maybe theoretical), which, if meticulously followed, can distinguish conjecture from knowledge. Of course, the way this is done will vary from discipline to discipline, but it is an essential part of the practice of science that there be methodological procedures in place for recognizing (or producing) knowledge. These procedures fall under the broad category of "scientific method," yet the details of its specific use will be cashed out discipline by discipline.

The distortion of the epistemological goal of the sciences, not unlike the distortion that occurs with the ontological goal, happens when the goal is abstracted from a specific discipline of science and applied to a broad claim concerning the nature of *all* knowledge. The humble claim that "scientific disciplines attempt to delineate knowledge from conjecture within their respective disciplines" becomes "the only knowledge that we can attain is knowledge acquired from the sciences." This latter claim is the definition of *epistemological scientism* and, like ontological scientism, it has very little to do with the actual practice of science. In order to see how *epistemological scientism* is a distortion of the epistemological goal, lets take a brief look at W. V. O. Quine's naturalized epistemology.

W. V. O Quine (1908–2000) believed that it was impossible to justify our knowledge of the world by starting with our sense experience. Quine accepts David Hume's skepticism regarding our ability to justify by reason how we acquire the perceptions that we have. As Quine poetically stated, "The Humean predicament is the human predicament."[8] Rather than attempting to justify sense experience, Quine's answer to Humean skepticism was to give up on the quest of using sense experience as a foundation for science, and simply begin with science itself. He writes, "I am of that large minority or small majority who repudiate the Cartesian dream of a foundation for scientific inquiry firmer than scientific method itself."[9] Quine then specifically pinpoints the science of psychology as the starting point for his epistemology because he is primarily interested in the way that human beings gain knowledge of, and (subsequently) learn to speak about, the empirical world. Since psychology seems to be the natural choice for telling us how we move from the stimulation of our senses to the uttering of words, Quine finds this a natural starting point in which to ground his epistemology. He writes, "The stimulation of his sensory receptors is all the evidence anybody has had to go on, ultimately, in arriving at his picture of the world. Why not settle for how this construction really proceeds? Why not settle for psychology?"[10] Quine replaces the non-informative question of how we *ought* to form beliefs about the

8. Quine, *Ontological Relativity*, 72.

9. Quine, *Pursuit of Truth*, 19.

10. Quine, "Epistemology Naturalized," 75. Quoted in Arrington and Glock, *Wittgenstein and Quine*, 68.

world with the more informative attempt to answer the question of how we *actually do* form such beliefs.[11]

I noted above that Quine's work is a paradigm example of how the epistemological goal of science gets applied so broadly that all knowledge becomes relegated to the things that the sciences tell us. At first glance, it appears that Quine is using the sciences to tell us what exists. It may therefore seem more natural to categorize Quine's naturalized epistemology as an instance of *ontological scientism*. However, a closer look at his view of the nature of science reveals the epistemological orientation of his position.

Quine never believed that our current science was the only way in which the "world" could be described. In fact, he thought that there very well might be numerous incompatible theories all capable of describing the empirical facts of the world in an adequate way. This is generally referred to as the "underdetermination of theory by evidence" and is described by Quine as the possibility that "[p]hysical theories can be at odds with each other and yet compatible with all possible data even in the broadest possible sense. In a word they can be logically incompatible and empirically equivalent."[12] While we may desire that such theories actually be translatable one to the other, there is no reason to believe that this will be the case. The theories may end up actually being incompatible. Take the following suggestion offered by Quine:

> Might another culture, another species, take a radically different line of scientific development, guided by norms that differ sharply from ours but that are justified by their scientific findings as ours are by ours? And might these people predict as successfully and thrive as well as we? Yes, I think that we must admit this as a possibility in principle; that we must admit it even from the point of view of our own science, which is the only point of view I can offer. I should be surprised to see this possibility realized, but I cannot picture a disproof.[13]

If this hypothetical culture's science is indeed "radically different" from our own, there may be no possible way to adjudicate the differences that

---

11. This replacement of the "ought" question with the "is" question is what Hilary Kornblith calls the "replacement thesis." See Kornblith, *Naturalizing Epistemology*.

12. Quine, "On the Reasons for Indeterminacy," 179.

13. Quine, *Theories and Things*. Quoted in Bergstrom, "Quine, Underdetermination, and Skepticism," 339.

show up between their science and our own, or to show that deep down we are actually dealing with compatible descriptions of the world. We may have to admit that, since their epistemological norms (i.e., their science) are sufficiently different from our own, their ontological commitments may be different as well. It would also seem possible that the way we have contingently come to look at science within our own historical setting could have easily gone in a vastly different direction as well (making our "possible" science "radically different" from our current "actual" science), and if that possibility did occur, then our discussion of reference as well as our epistemology would also be different. But how different could science have been (or for that matter still end up being)? Quine does not think that this sort of question can be answered *a priori*. He writes, "Even telepathy and clairvoyance are scientific options, however moribund. It would take some extraordinary evidence to enliven them, but, if that were to happen, then empiricism itself—the crowning norm, we saw, of naturalized epistemology—would go by the board. For remember that the norm, and naturalized epistemology itself, are integral to science, and science is fallible and corrigible . . ."[14] Since "what there is" is coextensive (for Quine at least) with what science tells us there is, and since science could be (or could have been) vastly different, it follows that "what there is" could also be (or could have been) vastly different. Thus, Quine takes the epistemological goal of distinguishing knowledge from conjecture in a specific discipline and applies it universally across all contexts to conclude that knowledge is whatever science tells us it is. In this way he comes to his ontological commitments by way of his epistemology. This is why I take Quine to be a better example of *epistemological scientism* than *ontological scientism*.

EXPLANATORY SCIENTISM

The two uses of scientism mentioned thus far have been fairly invasive when it comes to their interaction with other disciplines. That is, *ontological* and *epistemological scientism* grant little or no cognitive value to the work of non-scientific disciplines since any acquisition of knowledge about the nature of reality (and what else is there?) comes solely from the sciences. This doesn't mean that other disciplines cannot have some sort of aesthetic appeal; maybe they can entertain us in the way that good

14. Quine, *Pursuit of Truth*, 20.

literature does, or inspire us in the way that a good poem or a stirring song might. These flashes of aesthetic appeal or inspirational bliss, while having some possible benefit, will be of little or no value when it comes to telling us about what is *real* or what we can *know*. The forms of scientism that give rise to such an attitude (i.e., *ontological* and *epistemological*), while representing the most common way that the term has been used, also represent scientism at its most extreme. There are, however, other ways that scientism shows up that are far less destructive to the work done in other disciplines.

Explanatory scientism is the result of bringing the scientific methods of a particular discipline to bear on non-scientific disciplines in such a way that the result is some form of conceptual distortion. Such conceptual confusions are the result of a misuse of the explanatory goal of the sciences. However, in order to see how this goal may be misused, it is best to start with how it has been successfully applied.

The explanatory goal of the sciences—defined as the claim that within the practices of the science, scientists frequently seek to help clarify and explain (or make more precise) some of the concepts used in other (traditionally non-scientific) disciplines—has had numerous historical success stories. In order to see this we need only think of the way that psychology progressed from a fledgling sub-discipline of philosophy to a respectable empirical science, aided in no small part by the experimental and methodological work of Wilhelm Wundt and William James. Other examples abound. We could cite the development of cognitive science out of the behavioristic psychology of J. B. Watson, or the way that educational research progressed by merging with the scientific work done in human development and neuroscience. Or, for better or worse (depending on who you are), we could even cite the way that textual criticism, archeology, and linguistics have helped deliver various exegetical improvements to the field of biblical studies. In all of these examples (and others as well), we can see how the sciences have been expanded to help clarify and push forward the work done in other disciplines.

What is interesting, however, is that while the sciences can be used to help clarify or refine certain aspects of traditionally non-scientific disciplines, it is still possible to leave other aspects of the discipline untouched by the sciences. For example, neuroscience is immensely helpful for understanding the physiology of memory or for understanding the chemical causes of depression, but the philosophical problem of human self-awareness (what many call the "hard problem" of consciousness) eludes empirical description. And, while certain uses of the sciences have helped pastors and biblical scholars discern the meaning of biblical texts, many biblical scholars are also guided in their studies by the fact that such texts are taken as sacred documents, used as guides for worship and social action, and viewed as a source for human inspiration. Similarly, while educational research may be based on the latest science of human development or brain studies, certain aspects of teaching, while effective, are not considered scientific. While mutual co-existence between the scientific and non-scientific aspects of a discipline is ideal, it is also the place where trouble is apt to occur. Walking the balance between science and art (or science and the humanities) requires one to know which concepts should remain in place untouched by science and which are most conducive to a scientific re-description. When this tenuous balance is lost some cry a foul claiming that scientific explanation has gone too far. Despite our comfortable relationship with scientific descriptions of the world, we need to know when to stop. Understanding the nature of this conflict helps us to get a sense of the meaning of *explanatory scientism.*

What leads to a misuse of the explanatory goal? One problem, hinted at in the introduction, is that there is a tendency within academia to grant a certain pride-of-place to disciplines that can either transform themselves into a science or begin to look more scientific. But this only explains the motivation; it tells us nothing about recognizing conceptual limits and confusions. For that we need an account that goes deeper than simple motivation.

In *Science Deified & Science Defied, vol. 2*, Richard Olson writes, "When we think of science as a cultural institution characterized by certain activities and habits of mind often embodied in concepts and theories, then we can imagine a number of ways in which science might interact both positively and negatively with other cultural institutions, including religion and politics." As I have already noted, the positive interactions abound. But what about the negative ones, what has gone wrong in those interactions? Olson offers an answer. He continues, "Concepts or theories derived from scientific activity may be incorporated into the subjects dealt with by other cultural specialists because they meet some perceived needs of those specialists, or they may be attacked and rejected by other cultural specialists because *they seem to challenge the conceptual structures or practical claims of their specialties.*"[15] Olson's suggestion is that a negative interaction is constituted, at least in part, by some sort of conceptual challenge, or what I have called a "conceptual confusion." Although not mentioned directly by Olson, I take it that the conceptual challenge could move in two directions. That is, it may be that science is seen as distorting certain concepts that are important to a discipline's identity or that a discipline, as it attempts to become more scientific, begins to distort certain integral concepts that are a necessary part of science. In either case, certain important concepts are being distorted as the putative interaction with science occurs. Some examples may help clarify this point.

Grammar and Games

By paying close attention to how language is *actually used*, rather than supposing that we already know how it must function, Wittgenstein believed that we could travel the path from error back to truth. Wittgenstein called this a "grammatical" investigation (more commonly, such inquiries are called "conceptual" or "linguistic" analysis). The goal in such an analysis is a careful delineation of the concepts in question, i.e., an account of how the concepts are used and the particular roles they play in a specific context. As Michael Forster writes, a grammatical study looks at the "rules which govern the use of words and which thereby constitute meanings or concepts."[16] This is why Wittgenstein said that "[e]ssence is expressed by grammar"[17] and that "[g]rammar tells us what kind of object anything is . . ."[18] Attention to grammar, the particulars of language use, enables us to delineate a concepts meaning and to determine the nature of the "thing" in discussion. Wittgenstein often compared these grammatical "rules which govern the use of words" with the rules that govern the movements in a game (hence his use of the term "language-game"). Much of the work of the later Wittgenstein consisted in pointing out the grammatical rules of various language-games, and noting, with numerous examples, the semantic (or linguistic) confusion that results when various uses of language are

15. Olson, *Science Deified*, vol. 2., 6. Emphasis added.
16. Forster, *Wittgenstein on the Arbitrariness of Grammar*, 7.
17. Wittgenstein, *Philosophical Investigations*, §371.
18. Ibid., §373.

conflated or run together indiscriminately. Wittgenstein thus described his method as an investigation that "[s]heds light on our problem by clearing misunderstandings away. Misunderstandings concerning the use of words, caused, among other things, by certain analogies between the forms of expressions in different regions of language."[19]

When an individual uses words (or places various words together) in a way that ignores the rules that govern the words use in their standard or "ordinary" context, confusion (or nonsense) often results. This confusion is referred to as a "grammatical error," and the philosopher's role, at least for Wittgenstein, is to point out when such grammatical errors have led to confusion in the way we think about things. Consider the following fictitious example.

Imagine that we set out to compare two games; say chess and soccer. We begin our investigation by carefully familiarizing ourselves with the rules of both games, noting their similarities and differences. For example, we may note that the allowable moves of pieces in chess and the allowable moves of players on the soccer field are both governed by specific rules. Or, we may point out that in both games there is the possibility that a chess piece can be removed from the board and a soccer player can be removed from the field (after a penalty or a substitution). More likely, if we are careful in our investigation, we would point out the vast differences that exist between the two games. After investigating the rules that govern each game, we would be less likely to mistakenly or indiscriminately run the two games together. We would, that is, be less likely to shout "check-mate" at a soccer game or scream "goal" every time we move a pawn. If we were thorough in our investigation of the rules, we would be competent to point out when the distortion of a rule was leading to a distortion of the game as a whole, because if enough of the rules of chess or soccer are transgressed, the game being played would no longer be the same.[20]

Now imagine that we take the time to learn the rules of chess, and, furthermore, even though we have a fairly good grasp of the rules of soccer, we feel (for various reasons) that it is not a very good game as it stands and that it could be greatly improved if we attempted to update it by in-

19. Ibid., §90.

20. Of course, we would not have to be proficient in the rules of both games in order to know that the rules of one were being distorted. All that would be required is for us to be proficient in the rules of the game that we seek to protect from distortion.

corporating some (or all) of the rules of chess into the game of soccer. In this case we may attempt to impose the moves of chess pieces onto some of the soccer players (while leaving others to move as they please), or we may try to make it the aim of soccer to gain a check-mate on the goalie, or make it a rule that a player leave the field when another player intrudes on their space (as happens with chess pieces). Now whatever it is that we are left with after we reinterpret soccer based on the rules of chess, we can be certain that it is not the game of soccer as we know it. The game may become a chess game played with humans, or it may become a brand new game (say "choccer"), but it will no longer be anything that we would recognize as soccer. Of course, the occurrence of this type of interaction is not simply found in the fictional relationship between soccer and chess, there are also non-fictional examples.

Science, Psychology, and Education

In the field of psychology a general distinction is made between the clinical (or therapeutic) practice of psychology and the more research-based (or experimental) practice that focuses on hypothesis testing. The approach that stresses the empirical side of psychological practice is sometimes referred to as the "evidence-based practice" (EBP) approach. Barbara Tanenbaum defines (EBP) as "the application of scientific research findings to the treatment of individual patients."[21] Sometimes, though not always, animosity develops between those who do empirical-based psychology and the clinicians who spend much of their time in therapeutic practice. Yale psychologist Alan Kazdin explains this rift when he writes that "[t]here is a well-recognized split within clinical psychology between research and practice in professional work, career paths, and training. The split has come into sharper focus with the development and evaluation of empirically supported, or evidenced-based, interventions."[22] The problem concerns whether or not it is feasible (or beneficial) for individual psychologists who practice in a therapeutic setting to allow their discipline to become purely empirically based. In this case the dispute is not simply between those who see psychology as a natural science and those who see it as a social science, but rather between those who desire an empirical take-over of psychology and those who think it is essential

21. Tanenbaum, "Evidence-Based Practices," 163.
22. Kazdin, "Evidence," 146.

to both use EBP *and* to maintain certain practices that are not amenable to empirical investigation. Tanenbaum writes, "EBP sets methodological standards that may delegitimize effective treatments, and when those are incorporated into health policy making, patients and the policy may be adversely affected."[23] Tanenbaum does not say that an empirical-based approach to treatment is ineffective, but rather that if empirical-based practices are left to expand unchecked, certain other aspects of therapeutic treatment would be delegitimized resulting in more harm than good. It is this type of scientific encroachment that is at the heart of the claim of *explanatory scientism.*

Another example, this time from the field of education, may help to clarify what is meant by explanatory scientism. The *No Child Left Behind Act* of 2001 stated that education should be guided by what it referred to as "scientifically-based research" (SBR). This term is defined in NCLB as "research that involves the application of rigorous, systematic, and objective procedures to obtain reliable and valid knowledge relevant to education activities and programs . . ."[24] The same section of the document also states that educational research should (among other things) be empirical, use data analysis to test hypotheses, be reliant on observation and measurement, use randomly controlled experimental (and "quasi-experimental") methods, present experimental findings in sufficient detail, and publish experimental findings in peer-reviewed journals.

These requirements represent a tall order indeed. In fact, what NCLB did was to demand that educational researchers become nothing less than empirical scientists. Some, however, have claimed that the results of education trying to look like a science have been nothing short of ridiculous. Robert McClintock writes, "Educational research accumulates in great, growing bulk, with all manner of contradictory findings, and no leverage by which to effect practice in any significant way. . . . Don't take it personally—I'm sure your research is great, but taken all together, educational research has become absurd, out of harmony with sound judgment."[25] Yet, McClintock's complaint could be rectified if educational research simply became more scientific. Some have claimed, however, that asking education to become more like a science compromises aspects of education that

23. Tanenbaum, "Evidence-based Practice," 164.

24. NCLB, sec. 9101 (37).

25. McClintock, "Educational Research."

are effective yet not directly in line with the requirements of NCLB. Thus we have the complaint that "NCLB's emphasis on scientifically-based research unduly narrows what can be construed as acceptable educational research."[26] Furthermore, it seems highly possible that there exists effective teaching that NCLB would consider inadequate, even though there is ample supporting "evidence" for its efficacy that does not conform to NCLB standards. In such cases NCLB and its overtly scientific requirements create a distortion of certain effective and excellent teaching methods. The encroachment of the sciences in this case creates a conceptual distortion in which methods of teaching that have proven successful are deemed substandard. This is an instance of explanatory scientism.

These examples show how the explanatory goal of the sciences may impinge on disciplines to the extent that certain concepts—concepts that are valued and cherished by some individuals—get either distorted or (possibly) eliminated altogether. But there is no *a priori* theory that can predict when such disputes will arise. *Explanatory scientism* only shows up in practice. There is no set of necessary and sufficient conditions in place that serve as a set of criteria by which to recognize its occurrence. The brunt of arguments both for and against the use of scientific procedures in a discipline will tend to come from those within the discipline itself. For example, if practicing therapists believe that the encroachment of "evidence-based research" distorts some of the central concepts of their practice, they may need to show how such distortions occur and why the scientifically based research ought to be rejected. Similarly, if teachers believe that something essential to teaching is distorted by the requirements of NCLB, the burden is on them to illustrate the conceptual distortion. Again, there is no such thing as an *a priori* argument to show that an instance of explanatory scientism has occurred; rather, this decision has to be made as disciplines engage with the sciences. What is important for our purposes, however, is that at the heart of *explanatory scientism* lies the claim of conceptual confusion.

RELIGIOUS SCIENTISM

As we have seen above, *explanatory scientism* can occur in many different disciplines. My goal in the chapters that follow is to show how a certain misuse of the explanatory goal of the sciences has become the dominant

26. Liston et al., "NCLB and Scientifically-Based Research," 100.

approach in the academic study of the relationship between science and religion. A multitude of conceptual distortions reveal numerous instances of *explanatory scientism*. Since these distortions are prevalent in the academic study of religion, I have chosen to call the practice that leads to them *religious scientism*. In this case *religious scientism* is best understood as a subset of *explanatory scientism*; it is *explanatory scientism* showing up in the study of religion (and/or theology).

Smedes, Scientism, and Religion

While most of my thinking on religious scientism is the result of studying under D. Z. Phillips and reading the work of Wittgenstein, I have found that much of what I have to say on this topic also has a great deal in common with the work of Taede Smedes. As far as I can tell, Smedes (as well as possibly Andrew Porter) was one of the first individuals to overtly apply the concept of "scientism" to particular contemporary individuals writing in science and religion. While I have a few minor methodological differences with Smedes that are not (for the most part) of concern here, I am in general agreement with his project and much of my work is indebted to the work he has done on this topic. That being said, I will discuss two minor points of disagreement with Smedes that should further clarify what I mean by *religious scientism*.

First, Smedes, in my view, does not precisely capture the nature of scientism when he applies this concept to the work of certain theologians. He writes, "When I use the term 'scientism,' I refer to *that way of thinking and that attitude towards reality that is grounded in a scientific worldview*."[27] Earlier in the book he writes, "I describe scientism as a *cultural mode of thinking*, or an ideology."[28] While I do think, as I mentioned in the introduction, that there is a certain academic deference to science that creates the conditions for scientism, I do not think that scientism can be defined as simply an attitude, ideology, or way of thinking. I believe that our common academic culture has a tendency to extend the sciences in various ways, but whether this develops into a form of scientism depends on the specifics of that extension. As I have noted again and again, there is nothing illicit about the goals of the sciences unless and until they are extended and used in an illicit manner leading to conceptual confusions.

27. Smedes, *Chaos, Complexity*, 208. Emphasis in the original.
28. Ibid., 208. Emphasis in the original.

What Smedes describes as scientism could be construed as the very beginnings of extending the sciences; however, such a practice still leaves room for judging whether the extension is helpful or not. If not helpful, then the attempted extension could be withdrawn. In that case we have a "way of thinking . . . that is grounded in a scientific worldview" but no occurrence of scientism. So while there may be a way of showing that a certain attitude toward (or undue respect for) science lays the foundation for the possibility of scientism, Smedes' "way of thinking" does not capture the essential character of scientism, that is, its production of conceptual confusion.

Second, Smedes, at times, seems tempted to yield to a form of religious scientism himself. In *Chaos, Complexity and God*, Smedes argues that certain contemporary attempts to make sense of divine action are tainted by a particular reverence for the natural sciences. This reverence leads to an account of divine action that mixes up the language of science and the language of religion to create a category mistake (or what I have referred to as a "conceptual confusion"). More specifically, Smedes focuses on the work of John Polkinghorne and Arthur Peacocke and their attempts to use chaos theory and complexity theory to show how divine action is compatible with our current scientific view of nature. Up to this point I am in agreement with Smedes's project; in fact, his complaint is very similar to my complaints about contemporary work in science and religion. The similarity is likely due to our mutual respect for the philosophical work of Ludwig Wittgenstein. However, Smedes falls short when he offers his own explanation of miracles in order to satisfy certain *naturalistic expectations borrowed from science*. In fact, there is a sense in which Smedes appears to fall into the same trap as those that he criticizes. This should be explained further.

In *Chaos, Complexity and God*, Smedes quotes a biblical passage that describes the various miracles that Jesus accomplished as well as the reaction of the people to these miracles. After relating these stories, Smedes writes, "Here one finds no 'theory,' for instance, about how Jesus or God accomplished this healing without breaking the order of nature. Nor does one find people investigating the matter to see if it really is a miraculous healing. All one hears about is the people's response to what happens: they marvel, are astonished."[29] I think Smedes is exactly correct in his

29. Ibid., 211.

account. It is in the reaction of the people to the works of Jesus that we see what a miracle amounts to. No theory is necessary in this case. A theory would have no place in such a story. The reaction of the people shows that they believe no explanation is possible. They have just witnessed the work of God. Seeking for an explanation would diminish the account of what had just happened: the power of God manifest. However, even in cases where there is a natural explanation for an event, someone may still react as if the power of God is being revealed, and this for them would be a miracle. This is because the *reactions* of individuals to events are essential to what we mean by a miracle, not whether the events are naturally explicable or not.

There are times, however, when Smedes seems to think that some sort of explanation is indeed necessary. He writes, "If God's action is incommensurable with creaturely action, this means that it is no longer necessary to say that in order for divine action to take place, creaturely action must somehow be suspended, for it is then acknowledged that God's action is of a different order than creaturely action."[30] Smedes removes the discussion of divine action from talk of physical causality, but he does not remove it from talk of "explanation." When Smedes talks as he does above, he is no longer stressing the reaction of individuals to events, but using God's actions in an explanatory way to explicate divine miracles. He even commits a long section to explaining how miracles are possible due to the fact that God exists outside of time. Given the religious individuals' response to certain events, Smedes seeks to show how a miracle is possible by appealing to the ontological existence of God. Smedes writes that "God and created reality are not competitive parties because their respective ontologies, strictly speaking, are incommensurable."[31] Smedes then looks to the concepts of "time" and "space" to show how God's action is different from creaturely action. However, in entering into the explanatory game, Smedes misses the point of a miracle and places God in the explanatory gap.

There is an important difference between stressing the reactions of religious believers to miraculous events and using God as an explanation for how a miracle is possible. D. Z. Phillips makes this point: "To say 'God did it' promises an explanation without providing one. Ironically, the philosophical cum theological mind, wanting to show that science

---

30. Smedes, *Chaos and Complexity*, 214.

31. Ibid., 215.

cannot explain everything, testifies to the influence of that same science by turning God into a super-scientist."[32] In Smedes' attempt to show the differences between talk of the physical and talk of the spiritual, he appears to leave religion behind and speak of God's action in terms foreign to religious discourse. God indeed becomes an explanatory theory that is supposed to give miracles a certain kind of sense given the type of object (i.e., God) that serves as their cause and ground. Smedes' account is short on *religious* explanations.

Characteristics of Religious Scientism

These objections do not mean that Smedes' analysis of scientism is incorrect or unhelpful. I have already noted that I am in deep agreement with much of what he writes. However, I do think that he has a tendency to fall victim to the very way of thinking that he is trying to argue against when he offers God up as an explanation. Noting these differences, we are now in a place to more clearly see what is meant by *religious scientism*.

First, *contra* Smedes' claim that religious scientism is a scientific worldview, I argue that *religious scientism* only shows up in *specific* examples where the use of the sciences creates conceptual confusion for particular areas of religion and theology. Second, verifying the presence of religious scientism involves demonstrating specifically where religious concepts are distorted by comparing the distorted use of the concept with its use in a religious context. This means avoiding the temptation to fall back into a scientistic style of talking about religious concepts. When Smedes begins to talk about God in a way that has some affinities with the use of "explanation" in science, he is failing to do conceptual justice to the meaning of religious language. This, however, gets him caught up in the very sort of discourse that he is criticizing.

THE WAY FORWARD

In the beginning of his brief essay entitled *Remarks on Frazer's Golden Bough*, Wittgenstein writes, "To convince someone of the truth, it is not enough to state it, but rather one must find the *path* from error to truth."[33] The chapters that follow are an attempt to do just this; that is, they are attempts to retrace the path that certain thinkers have followed. My aim

32. Phillips, "Minds, Persons," 59.
33. Wittgenstein, *Philosophical Occasions*, 119. Emphasis in original.

is not simply to stipulate that the current state of science and religion is *necessarily* confused, but rather to trace out the path of specific examples in order to locate clearly where the errors lie. In a sense I like to think that I am doing the work of a modern day Alice interrogating Humpty Dumpty. In Lewis Carroll's wonderfully whimsical adventure, *Through the Looking Glass*, there is a dialogue where Humpty is instructing Alice in the finer points of semantics. When Humpty uses the word "glory" in a way Alice doesn't recognize, she questions Humpty on his grasp of the English language. Here is how a bit of the dialogue goes:

> "I don't know what you mean by 'glory,'" Alice said. Humpty Dumpty smiled contemptuously. "Of course you don't—till I tell you. I meant 'there's a nice knock-down argument for you!'" "But 'glory' doesn't mean 'a nice knock-down argument,'" Alice objected. "When I use a word," Humpty Dumpty said in rather a scornful tone, "it means just what I choose it to mean—neither more nor less." "The question is," said Alice, "whether you CAN make words mean so many different things." "The question is," said Humpty Dumpty, "which is to be master—that's all."[34]

There is a real sense in which the contemporary discussion in science and religion has been dictated by a set of well meaning Humpty Dumptys. Not that they look like eggs or are precariously seated on the edge of a wall, but they are insisting that they can make words mean just what they choose. In what follows I simply want to point to various ways were this Humpty-like semantic imposition shows up in contemporary science and religion. Ultimately my goal is to show that, *contra* Humpty's claim to Alice, the meaning of words are harder to discard than one may have initially thought.

---

34. Carroll, *Through the looking Glass*, chapter 6.

2

Bringing Heaven Down To Earth

IN *GRAVITY AND GRACE*, Simone Weil warns us against the mistake of representing the infinite God in ways more conducive to finite things. She writes, "We have to be careful about the level on which we place the infinite. If we put it on the level which is only suitable for the finite it does not much matter what name we give it."[1] Part of Weil's warning, at least as I see it, is to get us to see the possibility that our worship of the infinite may in fact be a fairly straightforward example of idol worship. This isn't because we intentionally aim our worship towards the finite, nor is it because we fail to refer to the thing we worship as "God," "infinite" or "Highest One." The problem is, rather, that when some speak of God they belie the meaning of their words by treating the divine as if it were simply another finite thing-among-things. If indeed our worship is directed at such an object (and "object" is the correct word here), then we worship the finite *as-if* it were in fact an infinite being worthy of our fealty. Yet this is what is generally described as idolatry. Indeed, actions speak louder than words.

Something like the error that Weil points out occurs regularly in the contemporary study of science and religion. It appears when certain theologians attempt to draw a parallel between the way that models are used in science to describe the finite world and the way language is used in religion to describe the invisible God. Specifically, these theologians want to show a sort of methodological similarity between the way that science and religion speak about the unobservable. While these theologians still want to refer to God as infinite, their actions (as Weil's warning suggests) place God on the same ontological level as the finite entities that science

1. Weil, *Gravity and Grace*, 19–20.

investigates. The oddity of the entire project is that part of the motivation for their talking about God in such a way is a hope of making sense of the reality of God. Andrew Moore describes their reasoning when he writes, "Theological realists have been impressed by scientific realists' responses to empiricism and use many of their arguments to defend a realist construal of the unobservable realm in religion."[2] In placing God on the same epistemological level as the finite unobservable entities of science, however, the concept of "God" loses its religious sense; God is transformed from the spiritual reality described by believers to something more akin to an unobservable scientific entity (and who wants to worship that?).

In order to see exactly how the theological use of scientific modeling has led to a distortion of the concept of God, it is first necessary to give a broad account of the function of scientific models, paying close attention to how these models are used as epistemological tools that help garner access to the unobservable aspects of the natural world. After that we will look at the various senses of unobservability as they appear in science and theology. Finally, we will close our discussion by looking at what I take to be a more theologically appropriate use of the concept of models in theological discourse.

SCIENTIFIC MODELS

Most of us are familiar with models of some sort or another. If we haven't built toy models ourselves, we have certainly seen model trains around a Christmas tree or models of the Eifel tower in the trinket shops around Paris. These simple examples of replica models, of course, belie the fact that models used by scientists are generally much more diverse, abstract and complex than simple scaled-down replicas of the readily observable objects that populate our world. Most models in science are not actually constructed or built; rather, they are ways of coming to see some aspect of reality in a new and different way, often positing unobservable entities as part of this new way of "seeing." However, more than simply coming to see something in a new way, scientific models are often used as explanatory tools to help explain some phenomenon (or set of phenomena). It is the relationship between models and explanation that I want to look at more closely in an attempt to give a general account of scientific modeling.

2. Moore, *Realism and Christian Faith*, 42.

Scientific Models as an Explanatory Tool

In his paper "How Models Are Used to Represent Reality," Ronald Giere writes, "Scientists use *models* to represent aspects of the world for various purposes. On this view, it is models that are the primary (though by no means the only) representational tools in the sciences."[3] Yet how is such representation supposed to work? Or, more generally, how do models perform their explanatory function by means of representation? While a complete answer to this question for all models is quite difficult (and beyond the scope of this work), a beginning can be made by stating that a model explains something about certain aspects of the world by standing in as a *representation* for (or "of") something else; something that may be, but need not be, unobservable. This does not seem far-fetched, since all models, whether they are the scale-type models sold in hobby stores or the more complex types used by theoretical physicists, are necessarily *representations* of something else (this is what is generally meant when we call something a "model"). Even when the term "model" is used as a synonym for "paradigm example" such as in "model student" or "model citizen," there is still one thing (the example of the "model student") that is representing something else (the abstract entity called "the model student"). This may lead us to the following initial formulation of a model:

(1) X is a model of Y only if X represents Y.

This seems adequate on the surface since representation is a necessary condition for something being a model. The problem is that representation, while being necessary, is not sufficient. It is obviously true that not all things that represent something else are considered models. A lawyer represents a client, a team captain represents his team, and the space needle represents Seattle, yet none of these things can be said to be a model of what they represent. All of these things may simply be different uses (with different senses) of the word "model," but they do not function as representations in any way that catches the use of a model that (1) intends to capture. So, again, even if representation is a necessary condition for "modeling," it is clearly not sufficient. The concept of representation, as it is used when referring to models, still needs to be refined in order to rule out those cases where representation is present in the absence of modeling.

3. Giere, "How Models Are Used," 747. Emphasis in the original.

One way to further refine our definition is to add talk of a *similarity relation* that holds between the model and the things that are modeled. However, to simply mention similarity in general doesn't get us very far since any two things are similar in some (possibly trivial) sense. For example, any two physical objects are similar in virtue of the fact that they both occupy space, or that they both have mass, while any two colored objects are similar in virtue of being colored. What is needed is for the similarity relation to be spelled out in advance in order to avoid the types of trivial similarities just mentioned. With the similarity requirement added, a model (in the sense we are concerned with here) may be defined as follows:

> (2) X is a model of Y if X represents Y by being similar to Y in respect(s) Z1 . . . Zn.

Now since the (Z) condition(s) need to be stipulated by the one who develops and uses the model (where else would they come from?), this definition brings up an important point that has been hinted at but which should now be made explicit, and that is the fact that all models (be they scientific or otherwise) have a pragmatic aspect that is only brought out (or decided upon) by the user(s) of the model. It is the community using the model that specifies this pragmatic stipulation; hence, to learn to use a model is often to be indoctrinated into a community of model users. We may call such contextualizing of the *use* of models their "pragmatic" condition. The pragmatic conditions of a model are a spelling out of Ronald Giere's claim that the use of a model must take into account the fact that someone uses models for some specific *purpose*. Giere writes, "Since scientists are *intentional* agents with goals and purposes, I propose explicitly to provide a space for purposes in my understanding of representational practices in sciences."[4] If we now add the pragmatic condition to definition (2) we get:

> (3) X is a model of Y if X represents Y by being similar to Y in respect(s) Z1 . . . Zn, and, "S uses X to represent W [or our Y] for purposes P."[5]

This definition now not only includes reference to individuals and their intentions in using the model, it also adds a "pragmatic clause" making

4. Ibid., 743. Emphasis in the original.
5. Ibid. Emphasis in original.

clear the importance the "use" of the model plays in delineating the meaning of representation. This stipulation will again help to rule out cases of incidental (or trivial) similarities affecting the efficacy of the model. While such incidental similarities may exist, they will not be part of the stipulated pragmatic use for which the model was intended. It now appears that (3) represents a fairly adequate, and sufficiently broad, definition of scientific models that may serve to explain how models in science fulfill their explanatory function.

A Place for the Unobservable

With a general explanation of scientific modeling in place, we now need to see just how it is that the concept of unobservability fits into this account. As a part of some scientific theories, models are sometimes used to make reference to aspects of reality that are unobservable (for various reasons) to human beings. In this case the model will pick-out (or refer to) some aspect of the empirical world that shares some sort of similarity relation with the model. This creates a couple of epistemological problems that should be dealt with. First, what does the similarity relation between the model and the unobservable entity amount to? Second, how do we come to know (or believe) that such a similarity actually exists? These questions will be dealt with in turn

If a model is a model of something that is unobservable, it is natural to ask how similar the model is to what is being modeled. Since the theoretical models used in science are not meant to be exact replicas of what is being modeled, it is best to think of them as metaphors that have (or might have) some sort of analogical similarity in common between certain aspects of the metaphor and certain aspects of the unobservable world that the metaphor is supposed to be explaining. Part of the reason that metaphor plays an essential role in describing the unobservable is due to the necessity of relying on the observable to talk sensibly about the unobservable. Richard Connell notes the relationship between observability, unobservability and metaphor when he writes, "Because we must know unobservables through the medium of observables, our initial transference of the name of an observable property or entity to something that is unobservable *has to be a metaphor*."[6] But what is it that such a metaphorical description is trying to accomplish?

6. Connell, *From Observable to Unobservables*, 48. Emphasis in original.

In the broadest sense the metaphorical use of language is a way of construing one thing as if it where like another *in certain respects.* Metaphorical language allows us to think of things in new ways and to construe something that is unobservable as if it were, in some sense, like something that we do observe. Max Black states "[A] memorable metaphor has the power to bring two separate domains into cognitive and emotional relation by using language directly appropriate to the one as a lens for seeing the other . . ."[7] A clear example of a metaphorical use of a model in science is the billiard ball model of gas. In such a model, certain aspects of the behavior of gas in a container are said to be (in certain respects) *like* the behavior of billiard balls. In this case, we may say that the "billiard balls" serve as a metaphor for the behavior of the gas particles. The important point here is that the model is meant to be similar *only in certain specified ways.* The individuals using the model spell out which aspects of the model they take to refer to the unobservables and which parts are simply superfluous. In the billiard ball case, gases function like billiard balls in some ways, but are unlike them in other ways. Mary Hesse calls the features of the model that *are* meant to refer to what is modeled "the *positive analogy,*" the aspects that *are not* meant to refer "the *negative analogy,*" and the aspects of the model of which it is *unknown* whether they refer "the *neutral analogy.*"[8] In this case, our first epistemological quandary regarding how models model the unobservable is answered by a combination of the pragmatic clause offered in the account of models above and the metaphorical nature of model language. But this still leaves us wondering what it means to say that our model is successful in referring to what it is supposed to be modeling; it is to that question that we turn to next.

The second epistemological question concerns how we come to know (or believe) that a model is actually referring to something that is unobservable? The answer to this question, I believe, has to do with the way that scientific models are supposed to be answerable to actual empirical states of affairs.

Because of the fact that models are constrained by (or answerable to) the empirical world, we can safely say that they are not *simply* attempting to get us to think about the world in a certain way (although they are

7. Black, *Models and Metapors*, 236.
8. See, Hesse, *Models and Analogies*, 8.

doing that), for if we are thinking of the world in a way that is radically different from the way the empirical world is, this will show up down the road as our model fails to account for certain empirical facts. This type of empirical constraint is distinctly different from the use of literary metaphors, which essentially function free from empirical constraints. This is seen in the use of the phrase "poetic license" which describes the literary freedom to roam without worry about whether or not one is "accurately" describing any empirical state of affairs. Scientific models are generally dispensed with if they fail to explain empirical data, or, more generally, if they fail to account for a given set of facts. Furthermore, with regard to experimental data, successful models should be able to handle unexpected anomalies that arise as well as being able to successfully make predictions about future occurrences based on past explanatory success. Ernan McMullin, following Thomas Kuhn, refers to this as the "fertility" of the model.[9]

Fertility is a function of how well the metaphorical aspect of the model, experimentally and predictively, "fits" with what the model is trying to explain. McMullin writes, "What best explains it [fertility] is the supposition that the model approximates sufficiently well the structures of the world that are causally responsible for the phenomena to be explained to make it profitable for the scientists to take the model's metaphoric extensions seriously."[10] Without saying too much about the realist/antirealist debate, it seems that McMullin is correct. Whether or not a model is taken to refer to unobservable aspects of the world is seen in how well a model explains certain aspects of the empirical world. This, in turn, is constrained by how well certain aspects of the model actually get it right, which, in turn, is constrained by the world itself. A model that is said to "refer" to unobservable aspects of the empirical world is a model that "works," however, we can also be sure that a model will not work unless it refers (in some sense) to the world it is modeling.

With this brief view of the nature of theoretical scientific models in hand, we can now turn to the use of models in religion. Especially pertinent to our project here, is the way that some theologians have sought to use religious models as a way of achieving epistemological access to the unobservable God. Even more important is the claim that there exists

---

9. McMullin, "A Case for Scientific Realism." In Balashov, *Philosophy of Science*, 270.

10. Ibid., 272.

some sort of methodological parity between the way scientific models refer to the unobservable entities in the world and the way religious models refer to the unobservable God.

MODELS IN RELIGION

In the early to mid-1960s a number of theologians began to write articles and books with the goal of showing that there exists a certain amount of similarity between the way models are used in science and the function of certain aspects of religious language. Two of the earliest of these works were Ian Ramsey's *Model and Mystery*, and Frederick Ferre's article "Mapping the Logic of Models in Science and Theology." These early works set the stage for later individuals working in science and religion to continue to attempt to explain just how models in religion and science were similar. Included in this later group are books such as Ian Barbour's *Myths, Models and Paradigms* and Sallie Mcfague's *Metaphorical Theology*.

Of course, claiming parity is never enough, and, as with most things, the devil is in the details. The problem with what we might call "the parity thesis" is that there is not simply a single argument for similarity presented, but rather a variety of arguments. Oftentimes those writing on the topic are even quick to point out the vast differences that exist between the way models in science and models in religion function. For example, In *Religion and Science*, Ian Barbour writes, "Religious models have additional functions without parallel in science, especially in expressing and evoking *distinctive attitudes*."[11] In *Models and Mystery* Ian Ramsey writes, "A particular model in theology, by contrast with the scientific case, is not now used to generate deductions which may or may not be experimentally verified."[12] The question then arises why make the case for similarity at all?

Earlier, I quoted Andrew Moore as a way of showing why it is that some theologians turn to the philosophy of science to make sense of God's reality. Moore's claim was that certain individuals hoped to use the realism spoken of with regard to scientific unobservables to make a case for the realist construal of the invisible God. On this account the focus is on realism. While I think Moore's claim is correct, I also think that the concern with realism cannot be abstracted from the question of unob-

11. Barbour, *Religion and Science*, 120. Emphasis in the original.
12. Ramsey, *Models and Mystery*, 17.

servability. It may be, and in fact I believe it is the case, that much of the claim to parity does not so much rely on attempting to make sense of the reality of God as it relies on the fact that both science and religion seek to refer to unobservables. It is then in the context of unobservability that the realism question arises. Of course, being taken in by the similarity of words without investigating their meaning does not a good philosopher make (do they also confuse the Godfather with the Father of God?). That being said, there does indeed appear to to be a certain fascination with the fact that both science and religion attempt to speak about what is unobservable. Take the following as examples:

1. "[o]ne of the most intriguing aspects of the interface between science and religion is the use of 'models' or 'analogies' to depict complex entities—whether the entity in question is an atomic nucleus or God."[13]

2. "As Models of an unobservable gas molecule are later used to interpret other patterns of observation in the laboratory, so models of an unobservable God are used to interpret new patterns of experience in human life."[14]

3. "Neither science nor theology can give plain, matter-of-fact accounts of the unseen realities (quarks; God) of which each needs to speak."[15]

4. "The metaphors of theological models that explicate religious experience can refer to and can depict reality without at the same time being naively and unrevisably descriptive, and they share this character with scientific models of the natural world."[16]

These quotes make two things clear. First, at least some of the claims to parity rely on the fact of unobservability as this concept is used in science and in religion. Second, religious models, much like their scientific kin, are supposed to play an epistemological role in giving us access to the unobservable entity that is being modeled. In this case any argument against parity is going to have to look carefully at the concept of unoberv-

---

13. McGrath, *Science and Religion*, 144.
14. Barbour, *Myth, Models and Paridigms*, 49.
15. Polkinghorne, *Science and Theology*, 22.
16. Peacocke, *Theology for a Scientific Age*, 15.

ability and epistemological access as these concepts are used in science and religion. I will begin with unobservability and then move on to look at the epistemological claim.

SENSES OF UNOBSERVABILITY

William Krieger and Brian Keeley, in their discussion of the realism of Paul Churchland, pose the following question about the status of theoretical entities in science, *"What metaphysical sense are we supposed to make of the sorts of entities to which scientific theories make reference all the time, but which, for a variety of reasons, no human being has directly experienced with his or her own senses?"*[17] Krieger and Keeley then outline various reasons why it is that the unobservable entities of science escape our observation. For example, some things are unobservable because we are not sufficiently close enough to observe them. I cannot observe a star in another solar system. Other things are unobservable because we are not temporally proximate enough to them in order to observe their occurrence. I cannot observe the birth of Richard Nixon or view the extinction of the dinosaurs. Still other things are unobservable because we do not have the correct physiological makeup that would be necessary in order to observe them. I cannot simply observe atomic particles or watch cellular mitosis. Since the first two types of unobservability rely on our spatiotemporal location in relation to what we are trying to observe, we can refer to these things as *spatiotemporally unobservable*. Since the third type of unobservability requires that we have our physiology amended in some way in order to observe certain entities, we can refer to this as *physiologically unobservable*.

While this list seems to cover the various reasons why unobservable entities in science might be unobservable, it is incomplete as far as the concept of "unobservable" goes. While there are things that are unobservable because we are to far away, are not in the right place at the right time, or are in need of an amended physiology, there are also things that are unobservable *in principle* such that no change in physical location, temporal location, or physiological capacities would suffice to overcome the unobservable condition. In the case of these types of entities, they are unobservable because unobservability is part of what we mean when we speak about them. I cannot observe *justice*, the number *6*, or *God*.

17. Krieger and Keeley, "An Unexpected Realist," 176. Emphasis in the original.

Certainly there are things that represent the number 6, there are instances of justice, and there is worship of God, but none of these concepts are observable *even in principle*. It is part of the meaning of the concept of a "number," a "virtue," and "God" to say that these things cannot be observed. In this case I prefer to refer to these types of things as *conceptually unobservable*.

It may help to further clarify the three different meanings of unobservable by asking what would need to happen counterfactually in order for something that is currently *spatiotemporally unobservable, physiologically unobservable*, or *conceptually unobservable* to become observable.

Counterfactuals and Observability

In the case of things that are *spatiotemporally unobservable*, making the unobservable observable is fairly straightforward. For example, if there is a planet that is so far away that we cannot presently observe it, we can imagine being placed in a position where normal observation becomes possible. In this case a spatial distance is overcome in order to make the unobservable observable. In the case of something that is unobservable because we are at some temporal distance from the object in question, the unobservable would become observable if there were some way to bridge the temporal gap and either go forward or backward in time to the moment when normal observation could occur. For example, if I could go back to 1865 and be in the theatre in which Lincoln was shot, I could (in principle) be a witness to Lincoln's assassination, or, if I were able to go into the future I could observe the marriage of my great-great-great granddaughter (assuming I were to have children of my own).

Both the spatial and temporal counterfactuals require that the observer (myself in this case) be placed in a better spatial or temporal location relative to the entity that is currently deemed unobservable. In such a case nothing would have to be removed from or added to the world (entity-wise) in order for something that is currently unobservable to be observed; rather, all that is needed is a reshuffling of the individuals' spatial or temporal location with respect to things that already exist, have existed, or will exist in the future. We may state the counterfactual situation thus:

> *spatiotemporal unobservability* [counterfactual]: If x were in situation c at time t, then x would observe s.

In this counterfactual, c would be the spatial location and t the temporal moment that we would need to be in to make the unobservable state of affairs observable. S, of course, is the situation that is currently unobservable, but, in principle (with the requisite changes), observable. In the case of observing Lincoln's assassination, c would be the condition of being physically located in the theatre where Booth shot Lincoln, t would be being in that theatre at the moment the event occurred and s would be the event of Booth shooting Lincoln. However c and t are filled in for each particular case, it is important to note that no change in the physiological or sensory capacities of the observer need occur. The type of observation that we are interested in here is the observation that a human being with normal functioning sensory capacities would undertake if in the advantageous spatiotemporal location.

In the case of things that are *physiologically unobservable* we may still consider a counterfactual situation in which what was unobservable becomes observable; however, in such a situation more will be involved than simply shifting the spatiotemporal location between a normal observer and already existing (or previously existing) entities. Krieger and Keeley offer an insightful example of this type of situation. They ask us to imagine a scenario in which "a man hears a series of very loud tones of increasing pitch. He is with his dog, who proceeds to howl after every tone. At some point, the man is no longer able to hear the noises, but the dog continues to periodically howl, falling silent at some time afterward."[18] Now as Krieger and Keeley note, "changes in location or life span would not solve the problem, rendering the unobservable, observable."[19] What is needed instead is "a physiological change (called canine-o-plasty) whereby the hearing range of the human ear is increased to include the range of the dog."[20]

Now the counterfactual situation that renders the unobservable observable in these types of cases would have to mention a possible world that is somewhat different from the actual world; that is, something will have to exist in the possible world that does not currently exist in the actual world. The counterfactual situation is not merely the actual world reshuffled (spatially or temporally), but a world with something ontologi-

18. Ibid., 184.
19. Ibid.
20. Ibid., 185.

cally new added to it. In the case noted above, what is new is the fact that a human (via "canine-o-plasty") is given the ability to hear sounds it cannot hear in the actual world. We may summarize this counterfactual situation as follows:

> *Physiological unobservability* [counterfactual]: If *x* were in situation *c* at time *t* *with w*, then *x* would observe (or perceive) *s*.

In this case, what needs to be specified is what is added in the possible world that is distinct from the actual world that allows for the possibility of the unobservable to be observed (this is what *w* indicates). So, to continue with the Krieger/Keeley example, if I were in a possible world listening to sounds of various frequencies with my dog Annie on Wednesday, and if I were fully recovered from my recent canine-o-plasty procedure, then I would hear sounds that I currently cannot hear. This possible world may be identical to the actual world in all respects *except* for the fact that I have been surgically given a new capacity. In this case the unobservable state of affairs can become observable, but only if something new is added to the world. Of course, in some cases what is new is not as drastic as canine-o-plasty; rather, what is often needed is simply new technology. Even in these cases, however, something new needs to be added to the actual world in order for the unobservable to become observable.

In all of the senses of unobservability just discussed, there is no logical problem with spelling out the counterfactual situation whereby the unobservable becomes observable. Furthermore, these senses of unobservability represent some of the common ways that the concept is used in the natural sciences. However, in the case of *conceptual unobservability*, things appear to be different.

God and Counterfactual Observability

It is a common and indeed necessary aspect of religious language to affirm the fact that God is not only unobservable but, as a spiritual reality, invisible as well. The question is how we should understand such an idea. If God were spatiotemporally unobservable, then we would be able to spell out a counterfactual situation which places the observer closer to God making God observable to our natural senses. But it does not make any sense to think that God is simply spatially distant from human observers unless we think that God is an object with an exact spatial location. In such a case we could attach a tape measure to God and see how far God lives from Pittsburgh; however, I take it that most people would think this is simply nonsense. All references to spatial distance takes place with reference to something else that is part of the universe; it is in this context that spatial distance makes sense. But what sense would it make to say that God is *spatially* distant from us yet exists outside the universe? If God is not another thing-among-things, not even a thing that is very far away, then the use of *outside* cannot have the same meaning it has when comparing the spatial relationship that one physical object has to another.

Something similar is true of trying to temporally overcome the unobservability of God. Since God is invisible and eternal, there is no sense to trying to imagine observing God by going backward or forward in time. No matter how much we imagine changing our temporal location, we will never be in a more advantageous position to observe God.

If God's unobservability is not similar to *spatiotemporal unobservability*, then maybe it is better seen as an instance of *physiological unobservability*. That is, maybe we could think of a counterfactual situation whereby human physiology is changed to such an extent that the unobservable God becomes observable. If it is the case that our current inability to observe God is simply a contingent fact caused by our limited physiological constitution, then maybe this problem could be overcome by adding something new to our current sensory capacities. It may be that some religious believers think that after death there are certain changes that will occur to the human physical make-up such that they will have the ability to observe God in heaven (maybe a type of "God-o-plasty" occurs). If this were possible, then we should be able to spell out the counterfactual situation that involves a change in our current physiological capacities that would result in making the unobservable God observable.

There are various problems with trying to overcome the unobservability of God this way. First, we need to remember that the type of changes needed to make the unobservable observable in the sense of *physiological unobservability* are changes made to *human* physiology that produce the ability to observe what was at one time unobservable. The point is that all of the examples of overcoming various unobservable situations, according to *physiological unobservability*, involve adding something new to our *current* physiological makeup in order to observe something that is itself physical. This presents a couple of problems when it comes to thinking of a counterfactual that would explain how we could come to observe God.

First, all of the counterfactuals above involve thinking of adding something to our current physiology so that we can observe something that is currently unobservable. However, in thinking about observing God, believers are usually talking about being with God after death. That is, in order to observe God one must first die so as to be sufficiently changed into the type of being capable of such observation. There are certainly no unobservables in science requiring that the observer first be dead in order for observation to occur! This fact alone renders the type of change needed to "observe" God vastly different from anything found in the sciences. Second, thinking of changing our physiological makeup in order to observe God makes the mistake of thinking of God as contingently unobservable. That is, it takes God's unobservability as something that depends on the type of physical creature we are rather than the type of being God is. This, however, is not what we mean when we talk about God being unobservable. God's unobservability is not something that is contingent. God being unobservable is built into what we mean when we speak of God as a spirit. God does not just happen to be unobservable, *God is essentially unobservable.*

By looking at just how different the senses of unobservability are in science and religion, we begin to see how the claim to parity ignores the religious use of language. However, one way to save the claim to parity is by attempting to point out similarities in the way that models grant epistemological access to unobservable entities in science and to the unobservable God in religion. In this case the parity shifts from unobservability *per se* to the epistemological status of models.

IN PRINCIPLE UNOBSERVABILITY AND EPISTEMIC ACCESS.

So far we have simply seen that God cannot be observed in the way that physical entities can be observed, and I take it that most individuals committed to the use of models in religion would agree. They may even retort that such parity is not what they had in mind in the first place. If there is going to be any hope for parity between the unobservable theoretical entities in science and the unobservability of God, then what is needed is a case where the entities of science are *in principle* unobservable. Andrew Moore writes, "When theological realists argue for reference to an unobservable God on the basis of an analogy with the referentiality of theory terms in science, they must ... maintain that *both* are *unobservable in principle*."[21] That is, we may be able to show the parity between unobservables in science and the unobservability of God if we can point to examples of things in science that are *in principle* unobservable. Such cases, if they exist, would be more like the unobservability of God since it would make no sense to offer a counterfactual that would render something that is *in principle* unobservable observable. Since it is here that the case for parity between unobservables in science and unobservables in religion is strongest, it seems worthwhile to pursue this a bit further.

It may be that there are things in science that are *in principle* unobservable such that it makes no sense to spell out a counterfactual situation that would render these types of things observable in either of the ways outlined above. It may be that such things as the inside of a black hole, atomic orbitals or dark matter are examples of *in principle* unobservability. In such cases when we infer the existence of these types of things, we do so on the basis of inferences made from certain types of observable data. We may call these types of entities "inferentially detectable." Even though they are not the types of things that can be observed, their existence can be justified inferentially. One may want to claim that the unobservability of God is more like these "inferentially detectable" entities and less like the unobservables mentioned above that can be rendered observable by spelling out certain counterfactual situations. That is, God may be *in principle* unobservable, but God is not undetectable; believers claim to detect God's presence all the time. In the way that certain unobservables in science are only detectable by inference from some observed fact, so the unobservable God is detectable by the observed fact of religious experience (or possibly the presence of miracles). While on the surface there does seem to be some sort of parallel here, it is not as obvious as it initially appears. We may be able to see the disparity clearly by looking at the lessons of John Wisdom's famous "parable of the gardener."[22]

In his essay "Gods," John Wisdom relates the parable of two men who return to a neglected garden only to find it filled with a combination of weeds and thriving plants. One man claims, due to the existence of the thriving plant-life, that a gardener must be responsible for tending the garden, and subsequently sets out to see if there is any evidence that would support such a claim. After realizing that the neighbors have never

---

21. Moore, *Realism and Christian Faith*, 65. Emphasis in original.

22. Wisdom, "Gods," 429–45.

seen nor heard any gardener working in the garden, the two men examine the contents of the garden more closely. Wisdom writes, "sometimes they come on new things suggesting that a gardener comes and sometimes they come on new things suggesting the contrary and even that a malicious person has been at work."[23] Both men see the *same* set of facts, and both men know what tends to happen to gardens that go untended. One, however, still assents to the belief in a gardener while the other stands firm in rejecting such a claim. Wisdom then writes, "At this stage, in this context, the gardener hypothesis has ceased to be experimental, the difference between one who accepts and one who rejects it is now not a matter of the one expecting something the other does not expect. What is the difference between them?"[24] Wisdom's parable is instructive for our purposes on several counts.

First, as Wisdom's parable makes clear, to detect God (or "The Gardener") is not simply to make an inference from evidence to fact in the way that occurs when there is observational evidence for an *in principle* unobservable entity (or process) in science. For example, when scientists note that a certain type of activity is occurring around what they think is the event horizon of a possible black hole, they move from that evidence to the claim that there indeed exists a black hole in that location. While there may be disputes about the evidence, there is little dispute that if the evidence shows that a massive amount of gravitational pull exists around the event horizon, then the existence of a black hole is justifiable. However, in the case of evidence for detecting God there is no such consensus. As Wisdom points out, individuals often see exactly the same set of "facts" yet reach vastly different conclusions about the *meaning* of those facts. This clearly indicates that "detecting" God contains a certain amount of subjectivity not found in the detection of entities in science. It is not that believers cannot offer reasons why they believe in God, it is just that what counts as evidence, while seen with equal clarity by both the believer and the atheists, is interpreted by each to mean quite different things.

Second, there is a certain amount of fallibility built into detecting things in science that is missing from cases where believers claim to detect God. More will be said about this shortly, so I will restrict my comments

23. Ibid., 434.
24. Ibid.

here to a few short remarks. Suffice it to say that in science there is generally a consensus around what types of evidence would count against the belief that a model actually refers to an unobservable entity. That is, if the evidence pointed in a certain direction, one would be justified in claiming that the unobservable does not in fact exist. In the case of inferring God from theological "evidence," however, there are no objective criteria that indicate when one should cease to believe in God. While there may be evidence that individual believers count as sufficient for ceasing to believe in God, this evidence is not objective in the sense that it is evident to all rational individuals equally. This is simply a way of saying that religious claims about the unobservability of God are not falsifiable in the same way as unobservable entities in science. Both this point and the one above indicate the way that unobservable entities in science are answerable to the empirical world in a way that is simply not true of claims about the unobservable God.

Third, when scientists move from evidence that some *in principle* unobservable entity exists as the causal explanation for some state of affairs (say the gravitational pull around the event horizon of a black hole), the claim is that the unobservable is something that is physical. That is, the scientist seeks to move from a certain set of data to a physical cause that would explain why the data is the way it is. In the case of detecting God, the tables are drastically turned. When believers move from evidence to the belief in an unobservable God as its cause (or explanation), they are referring to something that is non-physical. In the case of Wisdom's garden, if the men were to find a physical explanation for the condition of the garden they would cease to take seriously any claim that an invisible/intangible gardener was tending the garden. If a neighbor was sneaking out to tend the garden, or an alien was flying in on Thursday evenings to add fertilizer to the plants, then there would be reason to cease claiming that an invisible/intangible gardener could be inferred from the appearance of the garden. Detecting God is to understand that no physical cause can be inferred as an explanation for the way things appear. To say that one infers God from evidence is to say the opposite of what the scientist is saying: namely, it is saying that there is *no* explanation for the way the garden (or the "world") appears. This is what Gareth Moore has in mind when he writes:

The Christian does not *fail* to produce God, where he might have succeeded. For the Christian is committed, upon pain of idolatry, to rejecting any and every candidate that might be presented as the discovered God. . . . So it is not that he [the Christian] fails in the task of producing God. Rather, in Christianity, there is no such task. For the Christian is committed to finding what the atheist too expects to find—*nothing*. The disagreement between the atheist [and the Christian] does not lie here, in their expectations. Their disagreement is not like a disagreement over what might be the result of an experiment, what might be discovered, what might be apparent to the sense or register on our instruments.[25]

These three differences not only show that the use of *in principle* unobservability in science and religion is different, but also indicates just what this difference amounts to. In attempting to show some sort of similarity between *in principle* unobservability in science and in religion, one is committed to also showing that there is a univocal use of evidence in both disciplines. This, however, cannot be justified. The relationship between evidence and belief in science is vastly different than the relationship between evidence and belief in religion. This fact has more to do with what counts as evidence in each discipline than anything else. The mistake is to think that there is a univocal use of the term "evidence" in both disciplines. This seems to be the error of David Foster Wallace when he writes, "How can someone have faith before he is presented with sufficient reason to have faith?"[26] The answer is that it depends on what you mean by "sufficient reason." What we need to do is pay attention to what religious believers count as evidence (or reason) for their faith, not compare their reasons with those of the scientist. As David Berlinski notes in *The Devil's Delusion*, "The concept of sufficient evidence is infinitely elastic. It depends on context."[27]

RELIGIOUS MODELS AS REGULATIVE PICTURES

On the whole, there is nothing wrong with using the word "model" when referring to certain aspects of religious language. Rather, the problem is the importation of the meaning of "model" from the natural sciences to theology without any reference to the actual use that the concept has

---

25. Moore, *Believing in God,* 17. Emphasis in original.

26. Wallace, "Joseph Frank's Dostoevsky," 260.

27. Berlinski, *The Devil's Delusion*, 48.

in theology. This imposition of a foreign grammar onto religious terms creates the types of conceptual confusions mentioned in chapter one. If theological models are not simply epistemological tools meant to aid us in referring to an invisible spiritual entity, what is their function? While we may not be able to answer this question precisely (mainly because the functions of religious models are numerous), I want to suggest the following possibilities.

Religious models are ways of making sense of (or interpreting) human experience in relation to a life lived under the purview of the divine. In this sense, Barbour is partly correct when he writes, "As models of an unobservable gas molecule are later used to interpret other patterns of observation in the laboratory, so models of an unobservable God are used to interpret new patterns of experience in human life. Ultimate interpretive models—whether of a personal God or of an impersonal cosmic process—are organizing images which restructure one's perception of the world.[28] Barbour calls this type of interpretation of experience "interpreting-as" in a way reminiscent of Max Black's use of "construing-as," John Wisdom's use of "seeing-as," and John Hick's use of "experiencing-as."[29] Barbour's mistake is that in straining to relate science and religion, he is still attempting to show that there is a similar way that unobservable entities in science and the unobservable God serve to guide our thinking about reality. There appears to be an ever-present difficulty in giving up the superficial claim to parity and simply focusing on the uniqueness of the spiritual language that prompts talk of an invisible God. Since it is so difficult for some to talk about God without turning the infinite into something that looks strangely finite, I suggest that we simply quit talking about the relationship between God and models altogether. The problem is, as we have seen above, that in the scientific case the models of reality are constrained by the empirical world and by scientific experimentation. In the case of God the model points to nothing (in the empirical sense). The model is, so to speak, always before the religious individual's mind serving as a conceptual tool that helps give meaning to the believer's experiences and helps regulate their religious actions. In this sense religious models do not refer to anything, the model itself is the regulative picture that guides believers actions. As D. Z. Phillips writes, "[B]elieving in the picture means, for example, putting one's trust in it, sacrificing for it, let-

---

28. Barbour, *Myths, Models, and Paradigms*, 49.
29. Ibid., 51.

ting it regulate one's life, and so on."[30] This regulative use of a theological model (or picture) shows that the question of what the model refers to never overtly appears; however, this should not be taken to mean that the model can be reduced to a simple expression (or attitude) that one takes towards the world, for there are ontological commitments presupposed by such models; however, the *meaning* of these commitments is shown in the life of the believer not in some putative reference that the model makes. Again, the mistake would be to think that religious models function as a partial representation of the invisible God, when, in fact, the religious picture plus the believer's use of the picture is all we have. However, in saying this is *all we have*, I do not intend to suggest we need more. I am rather making the point that *a religious model gets its meaning in reference to how it is used* rather than by what it supposedly references. By turning theological models into a pseudo-scientific epistemological tool, we are missing the regulative point of the model entirely. The religious significance of seeing God in a religious model is exchanged for the scientific language of attempting to represent the unobservable God in the best way we can muster. This not only leads to a degradation of the meaning of scientific models, it also leads to a degradation of the concept of God. Religious models are regulative and not representative. They are existential and not epistemological. Here is how D. Z. Phillips puts the point, "The religious pictures give one a language in which it is possible to think about human life in a certain way. The pictures (and here one should bear in mind that 'picture' here covers related terms such as 'model' 'map') provide the logical space within which such thoughts can have a place. When these thoughts are found in worship, the praising and the glorifying does not refer to some object called God. Rather, the expression of such praise and glory is what we call the worship of God."[31]

I think this point can, and should, be made with much more urgency. The problem regarding the use of "models" and "pictures" of God arises out of the general need to talk of the term "God" as if it were a referring expression. If the spiritual reality of God, however, is to be taken seriously, then there is a very real sense in which we will have to content ourselves with seeing that *God is not the type of thing that exists*. This in turn means that religious pictures are not the type of things that refer to

30. Phillips, *Wittgenstein and Religion*, 65.

31. Phillips, *Religion Without Explanation*, 149.

God. The pictures *are* the reality of God. They *are* the physical expression of a spiritual reality. Borrowing from Wittgenstein on inner mental states: God is not a something, but not a nothing either. While thinking of God as not existing may seem a type of atheism to some, the alternative of thinking of God as a thing that exists is even worse; it is, as I said at the outset, a form of idolatry. In *Gravity and Grace*, Simone Weil writes, "Nothing which exists is absolutely worthy of love. We must therefore love that which does not exist. This non-existent object of love is not a fiction, however, for our fictions cannot be any more worthy of love than we ourselves, and we are not worthy of it."[32] I take Weil's remarks to be an instructive primer on how to think about God.

In much of his career D. Z. Phillips urged theologians to pay close attention to the religious meaning of the existence of God in order to avoid placing God's existence on par with the finite objects of the world. For the most part Phillips's request was unheeded, mainly because those who said they took him seriously also came to the conclusion that Phillips's grammatical work was actually reductionistic. While Phillips continued the battle until the end of his life, he may have been better served had he changed his tack. It may have been beneficial for Phillips if he had simply admitted that God did not exist. This would have freed him from the concern of trying to get others to see what the existence of God means. There is a certain tone-deafness to the grammar of God's existence that is propagated by continuing to use the verb "exist" when talking of God. The difficulty is not in seeing what a religious practice is, the difficulty is the constant desire to look behind the practice of religion for the divine cause that will grant us reasons for participating in the practice in the first place. But why not simply rest content with the reality of God being seen in the practice, period? The worry seems to be that this will lead to an insufficient reason for the practice. But if the reason for the practice is only seen in the practice, chasing an independent reason is a chimera. The difficulty is in following Simone Weil and learning to love the non-existent God.

32. Weil, *Gravity and Grace*, 163.

3

Designing Science

IN ONE OF THE most quoted, and most criticized, presentations of the design argument, William Paley writes,

> In crossing a heath, suppose I pitched my foot against a *stone*, and were asked how the stone came to be there, I might possibly answer, that, for anything I knew to the contrary, it had lain there forever; nor would it, perhaps, be very easy to show the absurdity of this answer. But suppose I found a *watch* upon the ground, and it should be inquired how the watch happened to be in that place, I should hardly think of the answer which I had given—that, for anything I knew, the watch might have always been there. Yet why should not this answer serve for the watch as well as for the stone?[1]

Paley's argument is that the watch is so intricately designed and obviously purposive that it could not have simply been lying around from all eternity. He then concludes that since our world resembles a watch in its complexity and purposiveness, it must, *mutatis mutandis*, have been designed as well.

Paley's logic is impeccable; at least when applied to artifacts like watches whose design is familiar to us. If I were lost on an island wondering if it were ever inhabited by intelligent beings and happened upon a shiny new pocket watch, I would feel justified in believing that the watch had been designed by some human-like being rather than thinking that it had been there eternally. In fact, the conclusion would be so obvious as to be hardly worth noting. Now the difficulty; the same thing cannot be said of the natural world. In fact, as Hume noted, in reflecting on the world around us we have no point of comparison that would allow us to infer that it was indeed designed. If worlds were as readily available and their

1. Paley, *Natural Theology*. Quoted in Pojman, *Philosophy*, 84. Emphasis in original.

design as easily attributable as human artifacts, we could forge ahead with Paley's example, but since our world is (at least for all we know) a one-off affair, Hume's argument against Paley's analogical reasoning is a better bet. Furthermore—and now for Darwin's dagger—the complexity that makes this world appear designed may simply be an illusion created by chance, adaptation, and a helluva lot of time. There may be a Watchmaker, but for all we know it may be the unintelligent blind version introduced by Darwin and popularized by Richard Dawkins.[2]

THE MODERN FACE OF DESIGN

Philosophical arguments, like bad habits, die hard, and the end of the twentieth century witnessed the beginning of a new type of design argument appearing under the heading of "intelligent design" (or ID for short). ID has distinguished itself from its traditional kinfolk in at least two important ways.

First, ID seeks (at least, in its official academic presentation) to remain neutral regarding any explicit theological commitments. In the more overtly theological versions of the design argument, including Paley's, the goal was generally to argue for a designer that was already part and parcel of a religious tradition or a philosophical system. Historically, this designer has been described as some sort of transcendent deity, whether this deity was the overly self-absorbed rational God of Aristotle, the mathematically savvy God of Isaac Newton, the intricate watchmaker of William Paley, or some sort of vague divine force that guided the process of evolution. On the other hand, the designer argued for in intelligent design is not intended to be the divine being of any specific religious or philosophical tradition. William Dembski, contrasting ID's goal with that of Paley, writes, "Paley's business was natural theology. Intelligent design's business is more modest: it seeks to identify signs of intelligence to generate scientific insights. Thus, instead of looking to signs of intelligence to obtain theological mileage, as Paley did, intelligent design treats signs of intelligence as strictly part of science."[3] In cutting design loose from the apron strings of theology, ID sets itself apart as an innovative version of the argument from design.

Second, ID presents itself as a thoroughly modern incarnation of the design argument not only by severing its theistic ties, but also by

2. See Dawkins, *The Blind Watchmaker*.

3. Dembski, *The Design Revolution*, 64.

presenting itself as a scientific research project. In seeing itself as a scientific research project, ID claims that there are some *specific* aspects of the natural world that are best explained by reference to an intelligent designer. In arguing that ID can explain these states of affairs better than any other current scientific hypothesis, ID desires to be seen as a competing scientific explanation rather than a theological argument. William Dembski optimistically writes "[i]ntelligent design is an emerging scientific research program. Design theorists attempt to demonstrate its merits fair and square in the scientific world—without appealing to religious authority."[4] Of course, all of this is just a shell of an argument waiting to be filled-in (which will be done shortly), but for now it is enough to note that ID is unique amongst design arguments in its attempt to be see as a part of science rather than a piece of theology.

These two characteristics together show ID to be an utterly contemporary phenomenon; a phenomenon that eyes science (rather than theology) as the most favorable battleground on which to fight for the efficacy of design. While ID comes in various versions with different aspects of nature serving as instances of possible design, in what follows I will focus on the argument presented and ably defended by William Dembski. Incidentally, a recent book with contributions from many well-known philosophers and theologians contains arguments that resemble the work Dembski has done in ID. Oddly enough the book does not even mention Dembski's name in the index (truly "[A] prophet is not without honor except in his hometown and among his own relatives and in his own household" Mark 6:4).[5]

In explaining the details of ID, William Dembski has at least three tasks to accomplish. First, he must *spell out the criteria* to be used if one is going to distinguish instances of design in nature from states of affairs that can be explained naturalistically. We will call this the "criteria condition." Second, Dembski must *explain why* such putative examples of design cannot be explained naturalistically. We will call this the "explanatory condition." Finally, he must show the *actual existence* of aspects of nature that qualify to be called designed. We will call this the "ontological condition." If these tasks can be accomplished, the claim is that we will then be able to point to certain states of affairs as indicative of design and be able to infer an intelligent designer as the best explanation for such

4. Ibid., 45.

5. See Davies and Gregerson, *Information and the Nature of Reality.*

states of affairs. In presenting Dembski's version of ID, each of the above three tasks will be dealt with in summary fashion.

In Principle Design: The Criteria Condition

Dembski poses the question of the criteria for design in terms of the *design inference*, which he states as an attempt to answer the following question, "if an intelligence were involved in the occurrence of some event or in the formation of some object, and if we had no direct evidence of such an intelligence's activity, how could we know that an intelligence was involved at all?"[6] What Dembski hopes to explain are the specific signs that we could appeal to if in fact an instance of design were present. It should be noted that Dembski is not seeking to index such indicators to *specific* instances of design (say, "A designed watch has indicators x, y, and z at time t"); rather he is seeking to explain what is common to *all* instances of design such that when we see those marks we can (with some degree of warrant) infer design. While he cites numerous examples where we readily make a design inference (archeology, cryptography, random number generation, etc.), his favorite example involves the movie *Contact* and its claim to have received intelligent communication from non-human extra-terrestrial life.

In the movie *Contact* (based on the book of the same name by Carl Sagan), SETI (Search for Extraterrestrial Intelligence) researchers receive a radio signal consisting of a series of 1,186 "beats" and "pauses" which, when written out in binary code (1s representing the beats and 0s the pauses), display the series of prime numbers from 2–101. The researchers infer such a signal cannot be random background noise or a beating pulsar (as was once the case), but rather must be intelligent beings attempting to make contact with humans. Dembski then asks, "What characteristic about this signal implicates design?"[7] He believes that if we can answer this question precisely enough, we may be on our way to explaining a set of criteria that would allow us to recognize design generally. Dembski then proceeds to answer his own question by stating "[w]henever we infer design, we must establish three things: *contingency, complexity and specification.*"[8] When these three conditions are met, the design inference is generated and a designed state of affairs is identified. Since these three

6. Dembski, *The Design Revolution*, 75.

7. Dembski, *Intelligent Design*, 128.

8. Ibid. Emphasis in the original.

conditions are jointly necessary and sufficient to implicate a designed state of affairs, it is incumbent upon us to look at each condition a bit more closely.

By contingency, Dembski has in mind the common definition of a state of affairs that obtains, but could have failed to obtain. The fact that I have on black socks today is true, but could have been different (I could have worn red socks or no socks at all); therefore this fact is contingent. In a similar fashion, the fact that Barack Obama won the election is also a contingent fact since it could have failed to obtain (if in fact John McCain had won). Rather than give a definition of contingency, Dembski attempts to explain the epistemological conditions under which one could verify an event as contingent. He writes, "In practice, to establish the contingency of an object, event or structure, one must establish it is compatible with the regularities involved in its production but that these regularities also permit any number of alternatives to it."[9] This way of putting contingency is a bit convoluted. To demonstrate contingency, all that is needed is to show the logical possibility that a state of affairs could be different than it in fact is. I take Dembski's way of putting contingency to be another way of saying that a contingent event (or state of affairs) is logically compatible either with an outcome different than the one that actually obtained or with no outcome at all. In fact, we can see this more clearly when we see the role Dembski assigns to contingency in relation to recognizing design.

On Dembski's account of freedom, a truly free act can occur only if it is possible for the agent who performed the act to have done something else (or nothing at all). Since a designed state of affairs is one supposedly brought about by the free act of an intelligent designer, the designed state of affairs must be contingent. For Dembski, then, the contingency requirement rules out the possibility that a designed state of affairs be the result of a necessary process, since any result brought about by necessity would preclude the possibility that the event was brought about by the free personal choice of a designer. Since Dembski believes necessity, chance, and design are exhaustive for describing any state of affairs, a contingent event rules out necessity and leaves the door open for design. Dembski writes, "Contingency assures that the object in question is not the result of an automatic and therefore unintelligent process that had no choice in its production."[10]

9. Ibid., 130.
10. Ibid., 128.

Next, Dembski's complexity requirement is meant to rule out the possibility of pure chance events being confused with ones that are in fact designed. For example, Dembski states that if the SETI researchers had picked up a radio transmission that revealed only the first three prime numbers through beats and pauses (instead of the first 101), they may have viewed this as random background noise and not evidence of extraterrestrial life. In this case we can see the complexity of an event is inversely related to its probability such that the more complex an event is the less probable that it happened by chance (or, conversely, the more probable it will be that it was designed). The complexity requirement, therefore, states that in order to infer design a state of affairs must be suitably complex in order to render its existence by sheer chance highly improbable. Now of course, as Dembski recognizes, "complexity (or improbability) isn't enough to eliminate chance and establish design. If I flip a coin 1,000 times, I'll participate in a highly complex (i.e., highly improbable) event."[11] In fact, no matter what the outcome of such a series of flips, it will always be a complex state of affairs that is the result of pure chance. According to Dembski, what is needed besides *contingency* and *complexity* is a way to recognize when a contingent complex state of affairs is an instance of design and when it is simply a matter of chance. The possibility of making such a distinction is the role Dembski assigns to the concept of *specificity*.

In order for a state of affairs to generate the design inference, it must fall within a certain specified pattern (possessing what Dembski calls *specificity*). Once again Dembski has a favorite example (borrowed from Aquinas) to bring home this point. He asks us to imagine an archer who shoots an arrow at the side of a barn fifty meters away. Surely the archer will hit the barn wall somewhere. But suppose after each shot the archer saunters up to his arrow and smugly paints a target around it after which she shouts, "Bullseye!" Despite the archer's bravado, what are we to infer from such a scenario? Dembski answers, "Absolutely nothing about the archer's ability as an archer. Yes, a pattern is being matched, but it is a pattern fixed only after the arrow has been shot. The pattern is purely ad hoc."[12] However, suppose a bulls-eye is painted on the barn in advance of any arrow being shot and the archer hits the center of the target eighty times in a row. Surely in such a case we would be justified in inferring that

11. Ibid., 130.
12. Ibid., 131.

we are in the presence of a world-class archer. Dembski uses this example to delineate three important components necessary for inferring design by using specification.

First, Dembski notes the need for a *reference class*. In the above example, the reference class is the class (or set) denoted by all the places on the wall that a possible (but non-specified) arrow may hit. The reference class then is represented by all possible positions of the arrow on the wall without regard to a specific arrow or an actual painted target. Of course, if enough possible arrows are imagined, the reference class would be co-extensive with the entire barn wall. However, if only one possible arrow is imagined, the reference class would be quite small. In compliance with the complexity requirement listed above, the reference class would have to have a certain amount of complexity (or number of possible arrows shot) in order to infer anything about the skill of the archer.

Second, the target that the archer paints on the wall prior to shooting any arrows sets what Dembski (and statisticians in general) refer to as the *rejection region*. The rejection region delineates the area on the wall that allows one to reject the chance hypothesis; the hypothesis that the archer continually hits the bulls-eye by chance rather than by design (or skill). Dembski states that in statistics the rejection region must be set in advance to avoid the type of *ad hoc* situation that takes place when a target is drawn around an arrow after the fact. Setting the rejection region in advance helps to avoid any "cherry-picking" that can occur as a result of looking at a data set and attempting to find patterns *ex post facto*. The specification requirement and the rejection region are linked in that the specification requirement is the actual setting of the rejection region.

Finally, Dembski's third requirement for specification is what he calls *detachability*. While Dembski agrees that in statistics the rejection region must be set in advance of any given event, this temporal detachability between event and rejection region is not always necessary. For example, Dembski notes that in cryptanalysis (or code breaking) the pattern is deduced after the fact, yet there is a pattern present making it possible to reject chance and believe that the code was the product of design. What Dembski does deem important regarding the setting of the rejection region (or specification) is that the event and the specified rejection region be independent of one another. He calls such independence *detachability* and describes it as follows, "Drawing a target around an arrow already embedded in a wall is not independent of the arrow's trajectory. Consequently such a target/pattern cannot be used to attribute the arrow's trajectory to design . . . Rather, to count as specifications, patterns must be suitably independent of events. I refer to this relation of independence as *detachability* and say that a pattern is *detachable* just in case it satisfies that relation."[13]

It is difficult to tell how Dembski desires to cash out the phrase "suitably independent" in the above quote. Much of the meaning is shrouded in the ambiguity of whether he means to take it as a metaphysical claim or an epistemological one. At any rate, the problem of specification and detachability is important enough that we will revisit it later.

The last component drawn from the archer's example is the actual event of a specific arrow hitting the wall. This represents the measurement of the precise location of every actually shot arrow. All such arrows will be a part of the reference class since they are possible arrow shots that have been actualized. The position of these actually shot arrows will be judged in relation to the rejection region (i.e., the target), and their position in relation to this region will determine if the shot is a candidate for triggering a design inference. Dembski notes that in order to infer design we must judge the actual position and size of the arrow against the size of the target. If the target (or rejection region) is so large as to include the entire reference class, it will be useless for inferring design. However, if the rejection region is small enough (and therefore hitting it is improbable) we can infer that an archer who hits it consistently (or with statistical regularity) can safely be inferred to be a skilled archer. Hence, the archer shooting the arrow in the rejection region (or the bullseye) with some regularity allows us to reject the chance hypothesis.

By suitably explaining his use of contingency, complexity, and specification, Dembski has given us a way of proceeding when we are attempting to decide if a specific state of affairs is indeed designed or not. What is further needed, however, is some way of explaining why it is that such states of affairs cannot adequately be explained by chance or necessity. It is one thing to say that a specific contingently complex state of affairs is indicative of design and quite another to say why such a state of affairs could not have been produced by chance or necessity. Some claim that evolution represents a prime example of how contingent complexity can arise from a purely random (non-designed) set of circumstances. It is this claim that Dembski addresses in what I call the "explanatory condition" of ID.

---

13. Ibid., 133. Emphasis in the original.

Filters and the Design Inference: The Explanatory Condition

With the above-mentioned guidelines regarding *contingency, complexity,* and *specification* (what Dembski refers to as the "complexity-specification criterion") in place, Dembski believes we have all the tools necessary to detect design. He summarizes his position when he writes, "There does in fact exist a rigorous criterion for discriminating intelligently caused from unintelligently caused objects. . . . I call it the *complexity-specification criterion.* When intelligent agents act, they leave behind a characteristic trademark or signature—what I define as specified complexity. The complexity-specification criterion detects design by identifying this trademark of designed objects."[14] Dembski presents the specified complexity criterion in the form of the following flow-chart which he refers to as the "explanatory filter":[15]

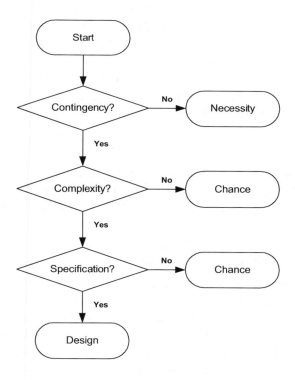

14. Dembski, *No Free Lunch*, 6. Emphasis in the original.

15. Adapted from *Intelligent Design: The Bridge Between Science & Theology* by William A. Dembski, 134. Copyright(c) 1999 by William A. Dembski. Used by permission of InterVarsity Press PO Box 1400 Downers Grove, IL 60515. www.ivpress.com.

Dembski's explanatory filter is a schematic for the specified-complexity criterion mentioned earlier. Each of the "nodes" in the filter represent points at which certain states of affairs are stopped and assigned to necessity, chance or design. To utilize the filter, a candidate for design is run through the start position and filtered down until it reaches a suitable stopping point. If an observation is not contingent, it stops at the first node in the filter and is chalked up to being the result of necessity. If it is contingent, but is not sufficiently complex, then it is stopped at the second node and relegated to the possibility that it was brought about by chance. The third node, as already mentioned, assures that no observations are labeled the product of design in an *ad hoc* manner, if the state of affairs does appear *ad hoc*, then it is also assigned to chance.

If indeed a state of affairs is able to pass all the way through the filter (exhibiting contingency, complexity, and specificity) then it is said to possess "specified complexity," and specified complexity, according to Dembski, is an accurate and reliable indicator of intelligent design. With his methodology for detecting design in place, Dembski's next challenge is to show that states of affairs actually exist in nature that can pass through the various nodes of the filter until the design inference is tripped. For just such a case, Dembski turns to the concept of "information."

Information in Nature: The Ontological Condition

Dembski defines information as an event whose actualization rules out other possible events. Explaining this further, he writes, "For there to be information, there must be a multiplicity of distinct possibilities, any of which might happen. When one of these possibilities does happen and the others are ruled out, information becomes actualized."[16] Now certainly all information is not created equal, since, on this construal of what information is, any contingent event will count as an instance of information. If I were to flip a coin 100 times, any combination of heads and tails will give us a certain amount of information (since it rules out other possibilities). In the case of information, (as in the case of the relationship between complexity and probability) probability is inversely related to information such that the lower the probability of an event the greater the amount of information involved. So a flip of the coin 100 times that came

---

16. Dembski, "Intelligent Design as a Theory of Information," in Pennock, *Intelligent Design Creationism*, 554.

up heads every time would contain more information than a 100 flip sequence that yielded thirty-seven heads. With the need to differentiate between trivial information states and the more interesting (and informative) type, Dembski fine-tunes his definition of information by applying the above-mentioned complexity-specificity requirement to the concept of contingent information states. When information is both complex and specified, it is referred to as *complex specified information* (or CSI). In fact CSI is a synonym for a state of affairs that is both complex and specified. It is the presence of CSI that Dembski believes initiates (or trips) the design inference, and it is also CSI that he believes cannot be explained naturalistically (i.e., by chance, necessity, or any combination of the two). So where is CSI supposed to be found in nature? One of the best ways to begin to locate CSI is to first attempt to distinguish "information" from the "matter" in which it inheres.

Dembski's distinction between "information" and "matter" is similar to Aristotle's distinction between "form" and "matter." For Aristotle, form and matter are separate, however they are not separable; form cannot be found walking down Broadway. Similarly, building materials do not make up a house until they take on a certain specified form. Aristotle also believed that a human being is made up of both form and matter with form contributing to matter both the "instructions" on what it is to become (its identity) as well as the "information" on how it is to proceed to become what it is supposed to be.[17] Dembski's concept of "information" can, I believe, be easily translated into something like Aristotle's "form." Dembski writes, "Matter is raw stuff that can take any number of shapes. Information is what gives shape to matter fixing one shape to the exclusion of others."[18] Information is simply the instructions that inform matter to become this rather than that.

From here Dembski's argument is fairly straightforward. He believes a certain amount—and possibly type—of information is needed for matter to move from dead inert stuff to living material. He further believes that the information needed for matter to transition from non-life to life is not found in the original state of matter; therefore it must have been added to the material system. But where did such information come

17. Of course, "information" and "instructions" are used a bit too loosely here, but even so, I believe the meaning is not too far from what Aristotle intended when he spelled out the function of "form."

18. Dembski, *The Design Revolution*, 130.

from? For Dembski the choices are four: chance, necessity, a combination of the two, or design. Dembski believes that necessity cannot generate new information, and while chance may generate new information it cannot generate the complex specified information that we see in living matter. Let's look at both of these claims a bit further.

Dembski utilizes "the law of conservation of information" (a term borrowed from Peter Medawar)[19] to show why necessity cannot generate new information. He writes, "According to this law, [of conservation of information] when a deterministic process operates . . . the amount of information that the process outputs can never exceed the amount of information with which it started. We might say it this way: *Deterministic processes cannot generate information.*"[20] The reasoning behind this claim is simple. Dembski asks us to imagine photocopying an out-of-print library book and then returning the book to the library while keeping the copy for ourselves. Do we now have any new information that was not already in the library book? Of course not! All that was involved was a law-like replication of already existing information. Here is the same point illustrated by another example.[21] Imagine a flat rock with the word "yes" painted on one side and "no" painted on the other (this is actually an image of the rock I used to ask my wife to marry me). Now imagine flipping the rock five times and getting the following results:

[series 1]: YNNYN (Y=Yes, N=No)

We can then apply this rule to each flip, "For every flip, turn the stone over and record the opposite letter." Following this rule, our initial series of rock flips becomes:

[converted series 1]: NYYNY

Now in the case of series 1 and the converted series, the bits of information have not changed. There are still five bits of information for each series of flips (assuming we define a "bit" as the letter assigned to each flip). This represents Dembski's claim that the application of a law does not create new information but, in a law-like fashion, simply manipulates information that is already present.

19. See Dembski, *Intelligent Design*, 170.

20. Dembski, *The Design Revolution*, 159. Emphasis in the original.

21. This example is a modified version of one offered by Victor Stenger. See, Stenger, "Physics, Cosmology and the New Creationsim."

Now, the "law of conservation of information" as stated above, fails to say anything about the application of chance to information states; its only concern was deterministic states. Dembski rectifies this problem by amending the law to include chance. He states the amended formulation as the claim that "*[n]either chance, nor necessity nor their combination is able to generate specified complexity or, equivalently, complex specified information.*"[22] We can illustrate Dembski's claim regarding the inability of chance to add new information by using my Stenger-inspired example regarding the yes/no stone. Again, imagine we get a series of flips that come out as follows:

[series 2]: YYNNY

We may then generate two more series of five random flips yielding the following:

[series 3]: YNNYN

[series 4]: NYNYY

Once again, it is clear in all of these series of chance flips that the amount of information in each series does not change (each series still has five bits of information). All that chance does is to rearrange already-existing information in a random way while adding no new information to the series of flips. To illustrate this further, Dembski asks us to imagine a typist randomly hitting keys on a keyboard. In such a case we may expect the typist to generate complex unspecified information, or, if the typist happens to randomly type the letters a-r-e, we may say that what is generated is specified information that is not complex enough to rule out chance; however, what we do not get is an instance of CSI.

By now Dembski's claim as applied to the biological world should be obvious. In the biological transition from non-life to life, new complex specified information (CSI) is added to the material world. This new CSI is what accounts for the transition from non-life to life. Remember, this information did not exist in the world of matter before non-life transitioned to life. Now, according to my interpretation of Dembski's argument, there are three possibilities to account for such new information: necessity, chance, or design. Since necessity rearranges existing information in a law-like manner and chance rearranges existing information in

22. Dembski, *The Design Revolution*, 160. Emphasis in the original.

a random way, the best explanation for the new information is intelligent design. Here is how Dembski describes the application of his argument to the biological world:

> In reproduction, organisms transmit their specified complexity to the next generation. For most evolutionary biologists, however, there's more to the story. Most evolutionists hold that the Darwinian mechanism of natural selection and random variation introduces novel specified complexity into an organism, supplementing the specified complexity that parents transmit to their offspring with specified complexity from the environment. In contrast the Law of Conservation of Information makes clear that without prior input of specified complexity into the environment, no natural mechanism, not even the Darwinian mechanism, will be able to produce specified complexity.[23]

In other words, if the CSI, which is present in biological life (and which was not present before the advent of life), cannot adequately be explained by chance or necessity (or its combination), then design is the clear and warranted inference we should make. However, this inference may be conceding too much.

It would appear that one of the more obvious ways to refute the claims of ID is to explain how (CSI) can be explained by natural processes (especially evolution) thus falsifying its design inference. The argument may want to show that simply because necessity by itself or chance by itself cannot explain CSI it does not mean that the combination of the two cannot. Maybe something like novel properties (including life) emerge when chance and necessity are allowed to interact on matter over time. In a way, this attempt at falsification would be the natural way to proceed *if you are willing to accept ID as a competing explanation for the origin of life*. However, prior to allowing ID the privilege of refutation as a scientific hypothesis, we need to examine its logical structure and see if ID should even be included into the domain of the sciences. In what follows it will be argued that ID's claim to be a viable part of science is suspect at best.

23. Dembski, *The Design Revolution*, 165.

AND THE PROBABILITY OF DESIGN
WITHOUT A DESIGNER IS . . . ?

With some qualifications, which do not concern us here, Dembski's argument is best seen as an inference to the best explanation. What Dembski presents is a certain type of abductive argument that utilizes the explanatory filter to adjudicate between possible explanations for the existence of CSI in the natural world. He has sought to show that ID is a scientific hypothesis that can explain certain empirical phenomena better than other competing explanations (including Darwinian evolution). In this case ID competes by comparison. When ID is compared with other scientific hypotheses that seek to explain CSI using chance, necessity (or a combination of the two), the claim is that ID fares best. Symbolically, Dembski's argument can be put as follows:

Design probability argument (DPA): $\Pr(O \mid ID) > \Pr(O \mid E)$

In (DPA), O = (CSI), ID = intelligent design, and E = evolution. This symbolic argument simply states that the probability of CSI existing given intelligent design is greater than the probability of CSI given the truth of evolution alone.

Now it seems to me that some serious problems present themselves on both sides of this probability statement. The first problem has to do with fixing the probability of the right-hand statement which sets the probability of O given E. It seems that how we fix the probability of the existence of CSI given evolution will depend on how we define evolution. E (evolution) can stand for evolutionary biology in its *current* state, or it can represent all the *future* possibilities of evolutionary biology that may come about as a result of the current state of evolutionary biology. Now if Dembski is arguing that evolution *in its current state* is incapable of explaining O, then ID is simply another version of the old god-of-the-gaps argument. ID becomes a mere explanatory stand-in for what science cannot *currently* explain. The various failures of the god-of-the-gaps arguments are well known and they not only stifle scientific progress (if taken seriously), but they represent bad theology. In general, the gaps usually get filled by science often leaving theology holding the bag and looking silly. However, Dembski may have something else in mind when he claims that the probability of O given E is low.

Dembski writes, "This [ID] is not an argument from ignorance. [Michael] Behe and I offer in-principle arguments for why undirected natural causes (i.e., chance, necessity, or some combination of the two) cannot produce irreducible and specified complexity."[24] Now what would such an "in-principle" argument have to accomplish to be success-ful? Dembski, it seems, has but two choices. First, he could claim that all future versions of evolutionary biology will be unable to explain O and that ID will continue to have the explanatory upper hand. However, without some form of omniscience regarding the future state of the natu-ral sciences, it is hard to take this claim seriously. Rather than an argu-ment from ignorance, Dembski offers an argument from omniscience. However, Dembski is probably arguing that since any future presentation of evolution will still rely on either chance or necessity (or again some combination of the two), and since these cannot explain CSI, there can be no future account of evolution that can adequately explain CSI. However, even in this case, Dembski is still over-extending his knowledge of how chance and necessity will combine with some future (and possibly un-discovered) facts about nature. Does he actually know that it is impos-sible for there to exist some future (but as yet unknown) combination of chance and necessity which will be able to sufficiently explain CSI? If he does know that, how does he know it? It seems that in both situations Dembski is creating a gap out of ignorance and then attempting to fill the gap by positing a generic designer as the best explanation of CSI. Even a scientific mind as powerful as Isaac Newton fell prey to such a tempta-tion when he argued that the best explanation for why all the planets or-bited the sun in the same direction was a divine explanation.[25] If Newton was proven wrong, there exists at least the metaphysical possibility that Dembski's fate may be the same.

Even with regard to the explanatory filter, Dembski seems to be op-erating from a place of ignorance for the following two reasons. First, the explanatory filter works by default. It is not that design plays a competi-tive role in vying for the explanation of CSI; rather, design is the best ex-planation when no other known cause is forthcoming. In this case, design becomes the ultimate placeholder where all events that are sufficiently complex currently tend to land. In this case, design has no explanatory

24. Dembski, *Intelligent Design*, 276–77.

25. See Newton's *General Scholium* that was added to the second edition of the *Principia*. See also Ferngren, *Science and Religion*, 154–56.

function in and of itself. Second, and related to the first problem, the filter is defective by virtue of the fact that it leaves no space for currently unexplained events to wait for an explanation. Missing from the explanatory filter, as John Wilkins and Wesley Elsberry state, is a "don't know" node able to hold the various states of affairs not currently explicable by chance, necessity, or some combination of the two, but possibly still in need of further investigation. Wilkins and Elsberry write, "If we can say of a problem that it is currently intractable or there is insufficient information to give a regularity or chance explanation now, then the Filter tells us we must ascribe it to design if it is specifiable. But it can be specifiable without the knowledge required to rule out regularity or chance explanations. This is clearly a god-of-the-gaps stance, and it can have only one purpose: to block further investigation into these problems.[26]

Now, since design is a default position with no real explanatory power, and, since the failure of necessity and chance are always temporally indexed to how these concepts function within our current practice of science, design is always the default position for a current gap in our scientific knowledge. In this case the explanatory filter is not a comparative hypothesis at all; it is a default node where "don't currently know" states of affairs are placed. There is no actual sense to be made of setting the probability of O given E except in an *ad hoc* non-comparative way since we do not know what the probability of O is until and unless we know what the future of E will look like; and this, we simply cannot know. You cannot get design by default.

Now what about the left side of DPA, or the claim that we can assign a value to the probability of CSI given intelligent design ($Pr(O \mid ID)$)? What exactly is the probability of O obtaining given ID? More poignantly, how do we figure out what the probability is? Elliot Sober believes that to make sense of the possibility of assigning a value to such a statement, we need to have some antecedent knowledge of the goals and abilities of the designer in question. Sober, writing in terms of Paley's claim that the human eye is evidence of a designer, writes "whether intelligent design has a higher likelihood than chance depends on what we are entitled to assume about the goals and abilities that the designer of the eye would have had if such a being existed."[27] Sober makes this point clear by using Paley's

---

26. Elsberry and Wilkins, "The Advantages of Theft over Toil," 716.

27. Sober, *Evidence and Evolution*, 142.

example of stumbling across a watch and wondering about its design. It seems fair to think that in stumbling across a watch we would be justified to conclude:

(D): "Pr(the watch has features G1 . . . Gn | intelligent design) > tiny."[28]

We may ask what it is about the design of watches that allows us to see it as trivially true that they are indeed designed? The answer, as stated at the beginning of this chapter, is that we are intimately familiar with both watches and watchmakers. We know enough about the goals and abilities of watchmakers to be able to determine that a watch is (was) designed. Now suppose we were to add the following background assumption to D:

(A): "If an intelligent designer made the watch, he would have wanted (above all) to *prevent* the watch from having G1 . . . Gn and he would have had the ability to ensure that the watch fails to have these features."[29]

If A is taken as background information to supplement D, then the probability of D becomes negligible because we have some more information about the designer in question. Every time we found a watch we would be in possession of a reminder of the watchmaker's miserable failure. Sober's point is that assigning a probability to the claim that a specified state of affairs is designed requires us to possess some sort of supplemental information about the designer itself. This is why the theological version of the design argument makes some sense, but it is also why the problem of evil is so compelling as well. This is also why Dembski's examples regarding inferring design from things like SETI signals and Mount Rushmore (another of his examples) are irrelevant when it comes to states of affairs that are utterly unique. Since, ID as a scientific hypothesis, would not be privy to any background information about the designer, setting the probability of O given ID is not possible.

INTELLIGENT DESIGN AS A CONFESSION OF FAITH

The above criticisms have all been aimed at ID as a philosophical or scientific argument that is supposed to move from some unexplained (or unexplainable) state of affairs to the conclusion that there exists an intelligent designer that explains the existence of that state of affairs. As men-

28. Ibid.
29. Ibid.

tioned earlier, the official position is that ID is not an argument for theism in general or Christianity in particular, but rather a scientific research program that offers the best explanation for certain states of affairs. The problem is that in divorcing itself from any religious context, ID either conflates into the old style god-of-the-gaps argument or is in need of independently defensible auxiliary hypotheses that can tell us something about the designer's goals and abilities. ID's problem is that it tries to covertly sneak a theological argument into the domain of the sciences while stripping it of the very thing that gives it sense. Oddly enough, it appears that ID can rectify its problems and reinstate itself as an interesting piece of theology, but only at the cost of overtly embracing the God it desires to hide. That is, if the argument of ID that was presented above is taken as part of the natural confessional beliefs of the religious believer, then the above objections can be avoided. In fact, if ID is understood as the natural stance a religious believer takes towards nature, it is easy to understand ID not as a scientific research program or even as a philosophically persuasive argument, but as a confessional statement on par with the religious utterance "in the beginning God created the heavens and the earth."

To state that ID can be salvaged—and not just salvaged but made religiously interesting—by coming clean about its religious commitments, is to get ID to admit to doing what Jennifer Faust calls "begging the doxastic question."[30] Faust writes, "An argument begs the doxastic question when a subject would find the argument persuasive only if she antecedently believes the argument's conclusion."[31] Putting the same statement in terms of the assigning of probabilities to statements in an inductive (or Bayesian) argument, Faust writes, "If an argument begs the doxastic question, then the assignment of some positive degree of probability to at least one premise [or probability statement] relies on acceptance of the argument's conclusion."[32] In assigning probabilities to arguments for ID and against evolution, defenders of ID are "begging the doxastic question." Of course this need not be a bad thing, it simply means that as believers, defenders of intelligent design tend to see certain aspects of creation as indicative of God's design. I refer to this type of ID as *confessional intelligent design* (or CID) since its adequacy relies on a prior confession of

30. Faust, "Can Religious Arguments Persuade?" 71–86.

31. Ibid. 80.

32. Ibid.

faith. If we rework the initial probability statements that made up (DPA) above, we get the following:

[confessional intelligent design: CID] Pr(O | CID > Pr(O | E&N)

In this statement CID = confessional intelligent design, O = CSI, and E&N = evolution attached to the presumption of naturalism, or the belief that nature is all there is. On this reading of the argument, the real foe of intelligent design is not simply evolution, but evolution *and* the philosophical claim that naturalism is true.[33] Attaching the "C" to "ID" amends ID to include its implicit theological commitments. Again, I call the above statement *confessional ID* because it flows directly and naturally from the confessional beliefs entailed by a Christian theistic view of nature. In fact, CID should probably be taken as the default position for most (non-deist) religious believers. It does not seem odd for an individual who believes "In the beginning God created the heavens and the earth" to also believe such creation exhibits signs of design; in fact, it would be odd if the believer did not hold such a position.

Now, can CID help us handle the problems attributed to ID above? I think it can since it allows the believer to firmly set the probabilities on each side of CID. First, take the claim that the existence of O (or CSI) is more probable given CID than given evolution and naturalism. Since a believer is antecedently committed to the belief that nature is God's creation, the combination of O given evolution and naturalism is going to be very low. Furthermore, the believer is going to assign a high probability for O given CID, not because it is a better explanation than other scientific explanations, but because the defender of CID is a believer. Furthermore, since a theist can spell out the goals and abilities of the theistic God (at least as far as their tradition presents these goals and abilities), they can also be fairly certain that the probability of the statement attributing the origin of O to design is higher than its attribution to the evolutionary process and naturalism. Now, rather than being an interesting statement of science, the high probability of O given CID and the low probability of O given E and N are best taken as the result of the confessional aspect of CID. It is the believers' way of seeing nature as created.

It seems that adding the confessional statement to ID can also help one escape the claim that the belief in design is simply another god-of-

---

33. This clash between religion and naturalism is the place where Alvin Plantinga identifies the real conflict between science and religion. See, Plantinga, *Science and Religion*.

the-gaps argument. CID does not depend on any specific state of affairs when it claims God designed the world, but rather on the (prior) belief that God is the creator of the world. In this case any way the world is described by the sciences will be compatible with the confessional statement that God is the creator and that the world is designed. There may be complex specified information that is not yet explained by science, but calling this designed does not depend on whether or not science can explain how it has occurred. The point is not that CID can explain certain states of affairs better than science, but that it is committed to attributing *all* that science investigates to God. CID can allow that science is incomplete and that future sciences may well explain O without worrying that this would falsify the claim that the world is (in some sense) designed. To confess that the world (as a whole or in part) is designed is simply to state that one sees God's hand in the world. What CID gives up is its competitive status as a scientific hypothesis, but since it is taken as a confession of faith and not a scientific hypothesis, this should not be bothersome.

Some may still conclude that admitting that the argument for ID rests on antecedent religious beliefs invalidates everything as trivial and uninteresting. However, the same might said about Anselm's ontological argument, Aquinas's five ways, and Alvin Plantinga's concept of a properly basic belief. Yet, these types of religious arguments, while not always philosophically persuasive and rarely of any scientific interest, are still religiously important. The problem isn't with the arguments themselves as much as it is with the expectations we often hold about what these arguments should accomplish. Wittgenstein writes, "A proof of God's existence ought really to be something by means of which one could convince oneself that God exists. But I think that what *believers* who have furnished such proofs have wanted to do is give their 'belief' an intellectual analysis and foundation, although they themselves would never have come to believe as a result of such proofs."[34] Now, if we can see ID as possessing the function that Wittgenstein applies to all such "proofs" (i.e., if we can see ID as an instance of CID), we may not be philosophically satisfied, and certainly science will pay ID no mind, but theologically we may be able to see ID's place as a theological reflection on the natural world.

---

34. Wittgenstein, *Culture and Value*, 85. Emphasis in the original.

4

On the Parity of Causes

Can Mental Causation Save Divine Action?

IN *CULTURE AND VALUE*, Wittgenstein writes, "A miracle is, as it were, a gesture that God makes. As a man sits quietly and then makes an impressive gesture, God lets the world run on smoothly and then accompanies the words of a saint by a symbolic occurrence, a gesture of nature."[1] Gestures, however, are not self-evident; as David Corner writes, "A human bodily movement becomes a gesture when it takes on a particular kind of significance."[2] We know when someone is making a gesture rather than, say, an inexplicable movement, because we have participated in the language game of gesturing. A miracle is not simply an inexplicably odd event, although some inexplicably odd (or even odd inexplicable) events can be seen as miraculous. A miracle *necessarily* involves a religious reaction to a particular event; it means *seeing* something as a revelation of the divine. An event without such religious seeing, no matter how odd, is simply not a miracle.

Peter Winch relates the story of a church in the South where some individuals began to claim that the statue of the Virgin Mother was actually weeping. Some said it had a perfectly natural explanation; others insisted it was a supernatural violation of the laws of nature. One lady, however, when asked about the event simply responded, "why would the Holy Mother not shed tears at the terrible spectacle of human life in our time?"[3] She showed no concern with whether the putative "weeping" was what science would describe as naturally explainable or whether it had a

---

1. Wittgenstein, *Culture and Value*, 45e.
2. Corner, "Miracles," §11.
3. Winch, "Asking Too Many Questions," 210.

supernatural source. To her the "weeping," *whatever its cause*, was of religious significance; that's what made it a miracle. Winch writes, "What was striking about the women was that she evinced no interest in the question about how what was happening might have been caused; and equally she had no interest in trying to show that it had no natural causes."[4] It isn't that the lady was intellectually lazy; it was simply that talk of causes and explanations played no role in the religious significance of the event.

It isn't always the case that one turns to religious language to talk about the meaning of miracles. Whatever merit the Wittgenstein and Winch accounts of divine action have, some still insist that the best way to account for the possibility of divine action is to look not to religion but to the natural world described by science. The fear is that a world that is tightly sealed by causal connections would be a world that is simply not conducive to divine action. Over the course of many years, Philip Clayton has attempted to make sense of divine action by attempting to give an account of nature that is ontologically open to the possibility of God entering into the world without demanding that such a Divine entrance violate any laws of nature. It is Clayton's "naturalistic" account of Divine action that will be the focus of this chapter.

WANTED: A NEW THEORY OF CAUSATION

Clayton takes the causally closed world described by the natural sciences to be an intractable problem for any account of divine action writing, "nothing in our explanation of science up to this point provides a way to make conceivable the idea of miracles in the physical world."[5] His claim is not merely ontological but also epistemological, since his conclusion is linked to a scientific description of causal closure, which, of course, is subject to change. He continues, "Because our knowledge of physics represents the most rigorous, most law-like knowledge humans have of the world, there is *never* justification for assuming the falseness of physics except in so far as one is arguing for a new and better physics."[6] The problem, at least as Clayton sees it, is that a causally closed world simply leaves no open crevices for the "finger" (much less the "hand") of God

---

4. Ibid.

5. Clayton, *Mind and Emergence*, 188.

6. Ibid., 188. Emphasis added.

to enter into a causal relationship with the physical world or its human inhabitants.

With the problem of the causal closure of the physical as his starting point, Clayton's strategy is to find a place within nature where such causal closure does not obtain. In essence he wants to find some type of ontological openness in the causal nexus of the world that could (in principle) serve as an entrance point for the divine. His belief is that what is needed is nothing less than a causal reformation. He writes, "Clearly, it is an urgent task for theologians to provide a clear account of what they mean when they assert God acts as a causal force within the world. *To succeed at this task we need nothing less than a new theory of causation.*"[7] Part of Clayton's error may be taking divine action as essentially causal; however, we will leave that aside for now. Clayton believes that if the natural sciences can yield an account of a causal exchange that is not physically closed and does not violate any laws of nature, then we may have a way of seeing how it is that God can interact with the world in a non-interventionist way.

Clayton's model for a "new theory of causation" is found in the seeming obviousness of mental causation; for example, when my desire for a drink and my belief that there is juice in the refrigerator is followed by the physical effect of my moving my body off the couch to retrieve the beverage. Here is how he summarizes his claim: "My thesis, in short, is the following: the question of God's relation to the world, and hence the question of how to construe divine action, should be controlled by the best theories we have of the relationship of *our* minds to our bodies—and then corrected for by the ways in which God's relation to the universe must be *different* from the relation of our mental properties to our brains and bodies."[8] It should be noted that Clayton is not attempting to find a causeless effect, but rather a type of causation that occurs while not breaking any natural laws. In essence he is looking for a type of causation that is natural but non-physical. We generally refer to this as mental causation.

Now while it may seem quite remarkable that the meaning of divine action should rely on our knowledge of how our mind interacts with our body, my purpose is not to criticize Clayton's method as much as to accept what he says and see if it can be cashed out in a philosophically meaningful way. The good news is that Clayton has offered us a fairly

7. Clayton, *Adventures in the Spirit*, 190. Emphasis in original.
8. Clayton, *God and Contemporary Science*, 233. Emphasis in original.

straightforward, albeit ambiguous argument. The claim is simply that in giving an account of how mental causation occurs we also garner a way of making sense of divine action. The bad news is that Clayton has hitched his theological wagon to one of the most notoriously difficult problems in philosophy (i.e., the problem of mental causation). But degree of difficulty is no way to judge the merits of an argument. With that in mind, the remainder of this chapter will be committed to presenting, analyzing, and criticizing Clayton's account of mental causation.

ON THE WAY TO DIVINE ACTION

In his recent book *In Quest of Freedom*, Clayton explains the problem that faces any individual attempting to make sense of mental causation when he writes, "The urgency of the question of human freedom has greatly increased in recent years, thanks to the growth of evolutionary psychology and to the new challenges that the neurosciences are raising to traditional theories of freedom."[9] What Clayton needs if his argument is going to work is a way of making sense of mental causation that can take the dependence of human mental states on the physical seriously while also allowing for a type of non-nomologically constrained human freedom. Clayton's proposal for offering an account of mental causation that can also be used analogically to make sense of divine action relies on the following three theses:

1. (*panentheistic thesis*): Theologically, we can utilize the concept of the "panentheistic analogy" as a way to make sense of divine activity (construed either as miraculous or persuasive).

2. (*emergence thesis*): The best way to explain consciousness is as an emergent mental property.

3. (*downward-causation thesis*): The emergent mental property of consciousness displays the causal capacity to bring about changes in the physical world without being nomologically constrained by the physical matter from which it has emerged.

We will briefly look at each thesis in turn.

---

9. Clayton, *The Quest for Freedom*, 12.

Panentheistic Analogy

As already noted, Clayton's argument proceeds by way of an analogical comparison between the relationship of our mind to our body and the relationship of God's actions to the world. This comparison he refers to as the "panentheistic analogy." While a discussion (and critique) of panentheism will be the topic of the next chapter, it is necessary to offer a minimal definition of panentheism here so we can grasp what Clayton has in mind when he speaks of the "panentheistic analogy."

Etymologically, panentheism simply means, "all is in God" (*pan=all, en=in, theos=God).* This is generally juxtaposed with pantheism, or the view that "all *is* God," and classical theism, or the view that God is utterly different than (and separate from) the created world. Panentheism is a way to view God as being immanent in the natural world while avoiding being identified with it (as is the case for the pantheist). Clayton, with some vagueness, defines panentheism as "the view that the world is in some sense 'within' God, although God is also more than the World."[10] Of course, the "in some sense" modifying "within" would have to be spelled out in order to get a clear grasp of what panentheism is actually claiming. However, for now, it is enough to note that panentheism is committed to some type of ontological (or possibly epistemological) closeness between God and the created world, a closeness indicated by the use of the prepositions "in" and "within." Theologically, such talk is generally referred to as "divine immanence."

Now for Clayton, the way God is "in" or "within" the world is supposed to be (again "in some sense") analogous to the way the human mind is "in" or "within" the human body. Or, to put the matter differently, the way the mind interacts with the body serves as an analog, *mutatis mutandis*, for how God interacts (or can interact) with the physical world. In fact, an oft-used panentheistic metaphor states that the world can best be seen as the "body of God." Clayton explains the essence of the panentheistic analogy when he writes, "Thus an analogical relationship suggests itself: the body is to the mind as the body mind combination—that is, human persons—is to the divine. The world is in some sense analogous to the body of God. God is analogous to the mind which dwells in the body,

---

10. Clayton, *Adventures in the Spirit*, 118.

though God is also more than the natural world taken as a whole. Call it the panentheistic analogy."[11]

We can symbolize the analogy in this way:

[*panentheistic analogy*] (PA): The B is to the M as the [(B+M) = (H)] is to G,

where B = body, M = mind, and H = human person (body + mind), and, G = God.

It should be noted that the analogical movement of the argument is supposed to be from understanding human actions to understanding divine action. Here is how Clayton describes the use of PA, "The power of this [the panentheistic] analogy lies in the fact that mental causation, as every human agent knows it, is more than physical causation and yet still a part of the natural world. . . . The panentheistic analogy therefore offers the possibility of conceiving divine actions that express divine intentions and agency without breaking natural law."[12] Even when we understand that the analogy is supposed to move from human minds to the divine action, there are still two ways of understanding Clayton's use of the panentheistic analogy. First, it may be that in giving an account of human freedom, Clayton is offering a possible preview of how the spiritual reality called "God" interacts with the physical world without breaking any natural laws (i.e., how God brings about miracles). Second, It may be that Clayton, in giving an account of human freedom, is showing how an ontological space is opened up (i.e., in the human mind) for God to causally influence human intentions without violating any laws of nature. While it isn't exactly clear which use Clayton favors, there does seem to be good reason to think he favors the latter. For example, he writes, "If human action is indeed non-nomological, divine causal influence on the thought, will, and emotions of individual persons could occur without breaking natural law. If (and only if) downward mental causation is a viable notion, could God bring about changes in individuals' subjective dispositions without negating the laws that we know to hold in physics and biology."[13] What is clear is that, on either construal of how divine action is supposed to work, the panentheistic analogy is integral to Clayton's account.

11. Ibid., 128.
12. Ibid., 128.
13. Ibid., 197.

Emergence

According to Clayton, emergence is the most scientifically feasible *via media* between conceiving of nature (including the mental) in purely materialistic terms and conceiving of it as dualistically composed of both mind and matter. Emergence allows us to think of mental properties as causally connected to the physical stuff from which they emerge without being identical to the emergent base. It also allows us to conceive of human mentality as being other than the physical without being committed to the dualism of mind and matter. Hence, emergence cuts a swath between mental reductionism and mind/body dualism. With such an important role assigned to emergence, it is essential that we get a clear idea of exactly what is being claimed.

In order for a property to count as truly emergent, it must have some fairly specific characteristics. First, it must be a property that is causally related to its emergent base, but which is also truly novel in the sense that it cannot be predicted from, or explained with reference to, the emergent base from which it arises. This also means that the emergent property is not reducible to the emergent base. We may combine theses ideas into what I will call the *novelty* requirement, which can be stated as follows:

> [*novelty requirement*] (NR): For any emergent entity *e* and emergent base *b* from which *e* emerges, *e* is ontologically distinct from (though causally related to) *b* such that *e*'s obtaining is not (and cannot be) fully accounted for (either predicted or explained) by simply listing the parts of *b* (and their relations).

Even though an emergent property is not reducible to, predictable from, or explainable in terms of, the stuff from which it emerges, we still need to give an account of how the emergent property and the base from which it emerges are related to one another. Generally, this relationship is spelled out in terms of the concept of supervenience that was brought into prominence (at least in philosophy of mind) by Jaegwon Kim. Since I will have much more to say about the various ways that Clayton uses the concept of supervenience, I will simply offer the following generic definition here:

> [*emergent supervenience*]: Property M emerges from, and is supervenient on, property B iff B is causally responsible for M and M is a novel property, meaning M cannot be explained or predicted in reference to the properties (or relations) of B.

On this definition, to say that the mind emerges from the body is to say that the mind supervenes on the body. Of course, this relation, as we shall see, can be filled-in in various ways. For now, however, we get a general idea about what an emergent property is if we combine the novelty requirement with emergent supervenience.

Downward Causation

What about the causal efficacy of emergent properties? If emergent properties are causally inert, then they are simply epiphenomenal having no effect either on other emergent properties or on the base properties from which they emerge. All of the causal work will be done at the physical level, leaving no room for the type of causal openness Clayton desires for his theory of divine action. Clayton resists this conclusion by differentiating between "strong" and "weak" emergence, the difference being that strong emergent properties are causally efficacious while weak emergent properties are causally inert (i.e., epiphenomenal).

Now up to the point of emergence giving rise to mental properties, strong emergence presents no serious problem since all the new emergent properties would continue to be physical, and physical causation (Hume aside) is not especially problematic. However, when a mental property is taken to be strongly emergent the story changes radically. Now the new emergent properties are ontologically different from the physical emergent properties that preceded them (and from which they emerged); hence, the causal exchange, according to strong emergence, will have to be different as well since it will now involve mental properties. But just how is this difference between the downward causation that takes place in physical emergent properties and those that are exhibited in mental emergent properties supposed to be understood? It is not enough to simply say what we get is "mental causation" without spelling out what this type of causation amounts to. How can a mental property cause anything to occur? This, of course, is the problem of mental causation in a nutshell; it is also the problem that Clayton has committed himself to solving in order to make sense of divine action. Just how he attempts to spell out mental causation and whether his position makes sense is what will be the focus of the rest of the chapter. Unfortunately, the main difficulty is in knowing exactly how to construct an argument that can be criticized.

THEFT OVER TOIL: CLAYTON ON MENTAL CAUSATION

In his *Introduction to Mathematical Philosophy*, Bertrand Russell wrote, "The method of 'postulating' what we want has many advantages; they are the same as the advantages of theft over honest toil."[14] In his recent critique of Clayton's emergent monism, J. P. Moreland applies Russell's criticism to Clayton's discussion of top-down causation (i.e., "mental causation"). Moreland writes, "Clayton's confusion is evidenced by the fact that he actually claims to provide an *argument* for top/down causation by merely offering a *definition* of levels that includes by fiat the notion of top/down causation. Unfortunately, this sort of 'argumentation' is what Bertrand Russell called philosophy by theft, not honest toil."[15]

The problem is not only that Clayton does not offer a clear argument for mental causation (as Moreland notes), but also that he is careless in his use of the concepts that are necessary if one is to try and construct a Clayton-like argument for mental causation. It is impossible to look at Clayton's various writings on the topic of the mind and not be struck by the ambiguities and inconsistencies that arise as he tries to make sense of emergent mental causes. Oftentimes Clayton's greatest enemy is not his argument *per se*, as much as his lack of consistency when trying to use concepts that already have a fairly clear meaning in the larger context of philosophy of mind. Therefore, as a prolegomena to attempting to construct a Clayton-like argument (or more specifically a Clayton-like explanation) for mental causation, it is first necessary to point out a couple of the more glaring inconsistencies that show up in two primary areas. First, there is the ambiguity that shows up as Clayton writes about the concepts of "strong" and "weak" supervenience across various publications and over a number of years. Second, there is the problem that Clayton seems to offer contradictory accounts of the relationship between what he calls the "neural correlates of consciousness" (NCC) and the possibility of human freedom. We will look at each of these difficulties in turn.

Strong and Weak Supervenience

I stated above that the generic concept of supervenience could be expanded in various ways. Clayton, following standard practice, distinguishes between weak supervenience (WS) and strong supervenience (SS); how-

14. Russell, *Introduction to Mathematical Philosophy*, 71.
15. Moreland, *Consciousness*, 149. Emphasis in the original.

ever, while using the standard labels, Clayton has a propensity to use these terms in a variety of different ways. For example, in his book *God and Contemporary Science*, he distinguishes between the two as follows:

> WS-1: "Take *weak supervenience* to be the view that it is sometimes justified to postulate mental properties without having to reduce them to their physical (subvenient) basis (e.g., Kim's position)."[16].

> SS-1: "*Strong Supervenience* would then be the view that . . . mental predicates can also have causal effects, effects not reducible to the physical effects occurring in the brain."[17]

In an article a few years later he defines these terms as follows:

> WS-2: "Suppose we define *weak supervenience* as the view that, although physical structures and causes may determine the initial emergence of the mental, they do not fully or solely determine the outcome of the mental life subsequent to the emergence."[18]

> SS-2: "We might call those views *strong supervenience* in which the physical determines the mental in its emergence and in all its subsequent behavior."[19]

Finally, in one of his more recent books, *Mind and Emergence*, he defines the same concepts in the following manner:

> WS-3: "supervenience means that one level of phenomena or type of property . . . is dependent upon another level . . .while at the same time not being reducible to it. I have used the term *weak supervenience* . . . as a way of expressing this minimal position."[20]

> SS-3: "*Strong supervenience* positions by contrast—and these are admittedly the most common—generally argue for a determination of supervenient phenomena by the subvenient level. This would mean, for example, that mental phenomena are fully determined by their neural substrate; . . . the 'strong' theory has to say that the subvenient level provides the real explanation for the phenomena in question."[21]

16. Clayton, *God and Contemporary Science*, 254. Emphasis in original.

17. Ibid. Emphasis in original.

18. Clayton, "Neuroscience, the Person, and God," 633. Emphasis in original.

19. Ibid. Emphasis in original.

20. Clayton, *Mind and Emergence*, 124. Emphasis in original.

21. Ibid., 124–25. Emphasis in original.

Clayton uses weak and strong supervenience in so many different ways that it is difficult to know how to make sense of his use of the concepts at all without indexing each use to the text in which it is found. However, we should attempt to clarify and summarize Clayton's various usages as a way to make the concepts beneficial for our discussion of mental causation. If we can combine the ways that he uses weak and strong supervenience into a sufficiently broad definition of these concepts, then we can begin to see how an argument (or arguments) for mental causation would proceed. Of course, without this possibility, Clayton's argument can never get off the ground. That being said, it behooves us to try and get a grasp on what Clayton might have in mind when he talks about strong and weak supervenience. Here is one attempt at elucidation.

WS-1 is a simple denial of reduction when it comes to mental properties while WS-3 both denies reduction and claims that a certain *dependency* exists between the supervenient property and its subvenient base. These two versions of WS say very little about the causal powers of the supervenient mental properties, leaving open the possibility that the emergent properties are simply causally inert. WS-2, on the other hand, states that while there is an *initial* dependence of the mental on the physical, there is also some possible future temporal moment when the mental takes (or can possibly take) on a life of its own and breaks free from strict dependence on the physical subvenient base. I take it that that is what is meant when Clayton writes that the physical does "not fully or solely determine the outcome of the mental life subsequent to the emergence." There is a certain tension between the dependency noted in WS-3 and the claim of independence in WS-2. The best way to solve this problem is to accept both that dependent and determine are synonymous and that either term can refer to a single initial moment or a series of temporal moments. On this way of construing "dependent" and "determine," a supervenient property may depend on (or be determined by) its subvenient base for a time while later taking on a life of its own, or, a supervenient property may depend on its subvenient base at all times that the supervenient property exists. We can further say that supervenient properties that depend on (or are determined by) their subvenient base across time may remain dependent on these properties for all of their actions (call this "full" dependence) or simply for their ongoing existence (call this "partial" dependence). In this case, partial dependence would allow WS-3, with its dependence condition, to still be able to make sense of mental causation since the supervenient properties may take on causal actions of their own while relying for their ongoing existence on the subvenient base.

With these clarifications, we can summarize a Clayton-like version of generic (WS) as follows:

> *(WS) Weak supervenience is committed both to the non-reducibility of emergence as this was outlined above, and to the metaphysical possibility that these non-reducible properties can take on a causal life of their own, breaking free from any determinative (or constraining) influences exhibited (at least initially) by the base properties.*

Now turning to Clayton's various uses of strong supervenience (SS).

In the above definitions of strong supervenience, (SS-1) claims that mental properties have causal powers not constrained by (or reducible to) the physical subvenient base. (SS-1) is oddly similar to the way Clayton talks about (WS). In fact, (SS-1) could actually serve as the generic statement of weak supervenience just mentioned. The problem, of course, is that Clayton's (SS-1) contradicts the definitions offered in (SS-2) and (SS-3). In both of these versions of strong supervenience there are straightforward claims that *no* causation occurs at the mental level by virtue of the fact that the mental is fully determined (in the "full" dependence sense) by its physical subvenient base. Since (SS-2) and (SS-3) state that the physical determines the mental, they are incompatible with any view (including (SS-1)) which allows for mental causation.

Because there is never an easy (or possible) way to solve a contradiction (short of trying to dissolve it), the best and most charitable thing to do is to interpret Clayton's various versions of strong supervenience over against his statement of (WS). If we do this, we may summarize a Clayton-like strong supervenience as follows:

> *(SS) The view that the mental is not only dependent on the physical, but determined by it to such an extent that all the causal work can be said to take place at the level of the physical.*

Nothing is lost if we simply set aside (SS-1) as an unfortunate rendering of (SS) and take (SS-2) and (SS-3) combined as our best summary of Clayton's various renderings of strong supervenience. With this amendment in place, and with satisfactory definitions of (WS) and (SS) in hand, we turn to the next area where Clayton shows a certain amount of ambiguity; namely, when he writes about the "neural correlates of consciousness."

Consciousness and Its Neural Correlates

In *Mind and Emergence* Clayton writes, "It [neuroscience] must not accept a definitional equivalence between brain and mind, an identity of mental states with brain states, lest the difference of the mental as we experience it be lost . . . but nor can it make the difference between brain and mind too great, lest the *obvious dependence* of mental states on brain states go unexplained."[22] We have already seen that the emergentist wants to reject any type of identity between the mental and the physical; however, it is equally important that the emergentist not deny the "obvious dependence of mental states on brain states." Of course, this dependence may be quite complex, involving some token mental state being correlated with some set of token brain states (which may differ, however slightly, from person to person), but what cannot be denied is that the mental actually has some sort of dependence on the neural states from which it emerges. We may call the claim that every mental state has a correlative brain (or physical) state "correlationism,"[23] and define correlationism as being committed to the following thesis:

> [*Correlationism (C)*]: For every mental state M there is a correlative brain state (or complex of brain states) B, and M depends on B for its existence.

The physical aspects of the brain that correlate with each conscious state are referred to as the neural correlates of consciousness (NCC) and can be defined, following David Chalmers, as follows: "An NCC is a minimal neural system N such that there is a mapping from states of N to states of consciousness, where a given state of N is sufficient, under conditions C, for the corresponding state of consciousness."[24]

Clayton elaborates on the importance of both correlationism and (NCC) when he writes, "If one is attempting to begin with the neurosciences, yet with an eye to the question of consciousness, there is an obvious place to start: with those data and theories that have as their goal to understand *the neural correlates of consciousness* (NCC). Following this

22. Ibid., 112 Emphasis added.
23. Thanks to David Chalmers for suggesting the use of "correlationism."
24. Chalmers, "What is a Neural Correlate of Consciousness?" 31.

method, one presupposes—as seems hard to deny—that consciousness is associated with specific neural activity."[25] The correlation that takes place between the state of consciousness and the brain state is not trivial, but is rather (as Chalmers notes) sufficient for bringing about the conscious state, or (as Clayton notes) it is the necessary condition for mental states existing. A trivial correlation, or non-causative correlation, would not be sufficient to bring about a conscious state, nor would a mental state depend on such trivial correlations for its existence. So when Clayton talks about a neural correlate of consciousness, I take him to mean that every conscious state (or mental state) has a corresponding non-trivial brain state on which the mental state depends for its existence. Clayton wants to spell out such dependence as a causal dependence; in what amounts to his clearest acceptance of the position I have called correlationism, Clayton writes, "These neural firings and action potentials, taking place in a brain with a particular structure and history, play a causal role in producing the phenomena of our first-person world: the experience of pain or sadness or knowing that 6 X 7 = 42 or longing for world peace."[26]

This all seems clear enough; however, there are times when Clayton does not see correlationism as being quite so obvious. In fact, there are moments when Clayton writes as if correlationism would make mental causation impossible. For example, he writes, "as long as supervenience is understood to be a *token-token* relationship—any individual instance of a mental property directly supervenes on some specific brain state [i.e. correlationism]—then, according to most standard presentations of the theory, there is no real place for mental causation. For in each case the mental event will be fully determined by its corresponding physical event, which means that the causal-explanatory story has to be told in terms of physical events alone (in this case, neurons firing)."[27] Yet, since Clayton wants to continence mental causation, he appears to be committed to rejecting correlationism. In order to save mental causation, Clayton at times denies any determinative role to the physical level. In essence he rejects (NCC). At one point he writes,

25. Clayton, *Mind and Emergence*, 112. Emphasis in original.
26. Ibid.
27. Ibid., 125. Emphasis in original.

I suggest that the explanatory power of the mental → physical causation is greater than those views that deny it. The result might look like this:

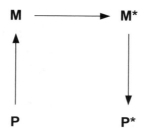

Here a brain state, P*, is caused by a mental predicate. This would be a genuine case of 'downward causation'.[28]

Now there are problems that the above picture of mental causation creates for Clayton that will be addressed shortly, but for now it is enough to see that Clayton thinks that any commitment to mental (or "downward") causation would mean that correlationism (even of the "partial" type) must be false. It would now appear Clayton has placed himself on the horns of a dilemma—either he must reject correlationism and lose the claim that his position is scientifically relevant, or he must accept correlationism and give up mental causation altogether. The best we can do is to utilize both correlationism and its negation when attempting to construct the various possibilities for a Clayton-like argument for mental causation.

VARIETIES OF MENTAL CAUSATION

With all of the groundwork behind us, we are now in a position to see the various accounts that Clayton might give of mental causation. Part of the difficulty is that Clayton's ambiguous use of the above mentioned concepts makes it impossible to formulate a single account of mental causation. However, it would seem the most charitable route to take is to begin with the assumption that mental causation is possible, and then use Clayton's different construals of supervenience and correlationsim to make sense of this possibility.

As far as I can tell, WS is incompatible with the truth of correlationism. This is because WS allows for the possibility that causal exchanges

28. Clayton, *God and Contemporary Science*, 256.

occur that are not controlled by brain states. This means there are possible mental causes not correlated with any brain state, rendering correlationism false. This would leave two possibilities open to Clayton. One possibility is to build a case for mental causation around the claim that strong supervenience is true. This would also entail an acceptance of correlationism (C), since, on Clayton's most recent (as well as his most used) rendering of strong supervenience (SS), every mental event is dependent on (and fully determined by) its physical subvenient base. The first possibility for making sense of mental causation, therefore, is the conjunction of SS and C, or:

(1): SS • C

Clayton's second possibility is to build a case for mental causation around the truth of weak supervenience (WS). WS entails both that mental properties are not reducible to (or determined by) the physical subvenient base from which they emerge and that strict correlationsim is false. Since WS is incompatible with C we get the following:

(2): WS • ~ C

Now since (SS) entails the truth of (C), and (WS) entails its falsity, these two options for making sense of a Clayton-like account of mental causation appear to be exhaustive. For reasons that will become clear soon, (2) will be referred to as an example of emergent dualism and (1) as an example of non-reductive physicalism. Clayton's argument for mental causation must, or so I claim, be equivalent to one of these two options.

The argument from here is fairly simple and straightforward; namely, it will be argued that the above possibilities force Clayton into either a dualism that he would find unpalatable, or into a version of mental causation that does not allow the ontological openness he desires in order for his account of divine action to make sense. Clayton is either forced to accept a dualism that denies correlationism and makes his view scientifically suspect, or accept a version of physicalism that leaves him still in the grips of causal closure. Either alternative, as we shall see, offers sufficient reason to doubt that Clayton can solve the problem of divine action by linking it with mental causation. The two possibilities will be analyzed in turn, beginning with emergent dualism.

Emergent Dualism

Option (2) above states that Clayton's weak supervenience (or WS) entails that C is false. This is to say that Clayton's construal of weak supervenience allows the possibility that the mental has its own causal powers not determined or constrained by the physical. As we have already seen, Clayton sometimes speaks as if this is the only way "real" mental causation could occur. In a certain sense, affirming WS and denying C represents another way of stating Clayton's commitment to strong emergence, which he defines as the belief "that evolution in the cosmos produces new, ontologically distinct levels, which are characterized by their own distinct laws or regularities and causal forces . . ."[29]

While this is certainly Clayton's position with regard to the mental, he is reluctant to refer to it as dualism. The obvious question at this point is why this view should not be construed as a type of dualism? One reason may be that emergence links the mental and the physical so closely together that dualism would seem unlikely. However, to think emergence rules out dualism is to construe dualism far too narrowly. Certainly Clayton's emergence would rule out Cartesian dualism with its focus on two ontologically distinct substances. However, dualism is certainly broader than Descartes envisioned. We may define dualism generally as the claim that the world is divided into two distinct types of properties (or substances): the mental and the physical. Now since two things being distinct does not entail they be utterly independent, there is no reason to think dualism cannot be couched in terms of emergence. In fact, since Clayton allows 1) that mental properties have causal powers that are neither constrained by nor describable in terms of the laws of physics, and 2) that mental properties are able to exhibit their causal powers independent of their physical base, there is reason to think that he is committed to some type of (possibly emergent) dualism. Since Clayton is countenancing two different kinds of things (i.e., the mental is not identical to the physical) each with its own unique causal powers, it appears that Clayton's commitment to emergent dualism is straightforward. In fact, this is exactly the type of dualism espoused and defended by William Hasker. Hasker states "[A]s a consequence of a certain configuration and function of the brain and nervous system, a new entity comes into being—namely, the mind or soul."[30] Now despite Hasker's use of the word "soul," he should not be

29. Clayton, *Mind and Emergence*, 9.
30. Green et al., *In Search of the Soul*, 78.

taken to think the emergent mental states (or "souls") are somehow in-dependent of the physical. He continues, "A strong point of this theory [emergent dualism] is that it immediately establishes a close connection between the mind/soul and the biological organism, a connection that in some other forms of dualism is far more tenuous. It prevents the split-ting of the person into two disparate entities and cuts off the implications ... that everything of true worth is to be found in the spiritual dimension and that the body is at best a tool, at worst an encumbrance for the soul."[31] So while Hasker, à la Clayton, admits that an intimate and dependent relationship exists between the physical and the mental, he is not shy (un-like Clayton) to admit that the disparity between the two warrants using the title of "dualism" (even if it is modified by "emergent"). So why does Clayton not admit to being a dualist? His reasoning is two-fold.

First, Clayton seems to be in the class of individuals mentioned above who want to limit dualism to Cartesian dualism. He writes, "Let's call those theories of emergence 'very strong' or 'hyper-strong' which not only (*a*) individuate relational complexes, (*b*) ascribe reality to them through an ontology of relations, and (*c*) ascribe causal powers and activ-ity to them, but also (*d*) treat them as individual substances in their own right."[32] He then equates the above criteria with Hasker's emergent dual-ism, stating that Hasker is committed to a theory of "substantival entities" which he [Clayton] rejects as being antithetical to his commitment to emergence. The claim is that Hasker begins as an emergentist and ends up as a dualist because he grants the mental the title of "substance." There are at least two problems with Clayton's reasoning. First, criterion (*d*) states that an emergent dualist "treat" relational complexes as "individual sub-stances in their own right." However, substance dualists do not just treat certain properties *as if* they were distinct substances, they believe they *actually* are different substances. In turning Hasker's emergent dualism into a form of Cartesian dualism, Clayton is ignoring the fact that on Hasker's account the mental and physical are causally linked in a way that Descartes would have denied. Second, there is no actual substan-tive difference between the positions espoused by Clayton and Hasker. While Clayton avoids calling the mental emergent property a "substance," Hasker avoids the possibility of thinking that the "substance" he speaks

31. Ibid., 78–79.
32. Clayton, *Mind and Emergence*, 16.

of is separable (except possibly after death) from its emergent base. So when Clayton writes that Hasker (or emergent dualists of Hasker's type) see the emergent mental states as "substances in their own right, almost as distinct from their origins as Cartesian mind is from body,"[33] he is hiding behind the "almost" qualification. In fact, it is the need for the "almost" qualifier that keeps Hasker from being a Cartesian dualist and places Hasker and Clayton in the same metaphysical camp. Hasker himself states that his granting the status of "substance" to the mental is partly due to the fact that the emergent mind has causal powers not explainable in terms of the physical brain,[34] something with which Clayton (at times) would agree. In this case Clayton seems to be a non-dualist in word only.

Clayton's second strategy for avoiding dualism is equally slippery. Clayton seems to think that if he places everything in the natural world under the broad label of "stuff" he has somehow stated an acceptable form of monism. This type of monism is what Clayton refers to as emergent monism. Here is how he describes his position, "Reality is ultimately composed of one basic kind of stuff. Yet the concepts of physics are not sufficient to explain all the forms that this stuff takes . . . The one 'stuff' apparently takes forms for which the explanations of physics, and thus the ontology of physics . . . are not adequate. We should not assume that the entities postulated by physics complete the inventory of what exists. Hence the emergentists should be monists but not physicalists."[35] However, calling the mental and the physical the same "stuff" is not an argument for monism but simply a catch-all phrase used to avoid dualism. So while Clayton defines his ontology to make it appear parsimonious, it actually, if we accept WS and the negation of correlationism, entails, at minimum, the mental and the physical. A dualist by any other name is still a dualist.

Emergent dualism would be able to solve the problem of divine action because it would offer a way for God to causally interact with the world at a place where causal closure does not hold; namely, at the place where our mental intentions are formed leading to subsequent actions. God could influence our mental intentions bringing about real changes in the physical world without breaking any natural laws. Of course, this tells us nothing about how it is that God influences our intentions or

33. Clayton, "Conceptual Foundations," 14.

34. See Hasker, *The Emergent Self*, 195.

35. Clayton, *Mind and Emergence*, 4.

about how mental causation is supposed to work. The problem, at least for Clayton, is that this view is scientifically unsavory. He writes, "From a scientific perspective it is preferable to explain mental causation by appealing only to mental properties and the components of the central nervous systems, rather than introducing mental 'things' such as minds and spirits."[36] Since emergent dualism is unacceptable, we need to locate a form of mental causation that makes room for the neurosciences. To see what this might look like given Clayton's previous commitments, we turn now to a discussion of a non-dualist account of mental causation.

Mental Causation Without Magic

The above option, which leads to emergent dualism, is not the only way that Clayton can make sense of mental causation. He may be able to avoid the (possibly) disagreeable conclusion that mental properties causally act without any aid from their physical base by accepting the conjunction of strong supervenience and correlationism (as he sometimes actually seems apt to do). He writes that "[t]he balance that we [emergentists] seek conceives mind as a type of property that emerges from the brain, which though different from remains continually dependent on its subvenient base . . ."[37] The difficulty for Clayton will be to allow mental properties causal autonomy while still maintaining that they depend on their physical base. At times, Clayton himself seems to not have appreciated this point. We saw earlier that he claimed that an instance of mental causation would look like the following:

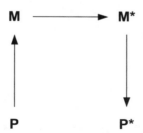

On this construal of mental causation, mental property M (which emerges from physical base P) directly causes mental predicate M* which in turn causes P*. However, if Clayton accepts correlationism, then he must

36. Ibid., 17.
37. Ibid., 128.

accept that the causal exchange between M and M* has a physical (non-trivial) correlate moving from P to P*. Now we get the following picture:

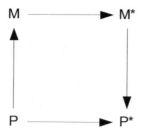

In this case M would serve as the cause for M* (which would then cause P*), and P would simultaneously serve as the cause for both M and P*. However, according to emergence, this picture is not possible since, as Jaegwon Kim notes, "[t]he only way to cause an emergent property is to bring about an appropriate basal condition; there is no other way."[38] That is, on this account, M* is floating free of any emergent base. This problem does not require an argument since it follows from the definition of emergence. We now have to modify the above diagram to take into account the fact that M must first cause P* in order to bring about M*. We now obtain the following:

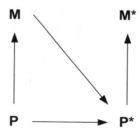

This is certainly a more accurate representation of what a non-dualist emergence account of mental causation would look like. In this case M causes M* by first causing its emergent base P*. However, according to C (or correlationism) there is also a corresponding physical cause for P*, namely P. While this picture captures the commitment to the conjunction of C and SS, it leaves Clayton open to a certain type of argument against

---

38. Kim, "Being Realistic about Emergence," 199.

mental causation that has been developed and made famous by Jaegwon Kim.

Kim writes that the problem of mental causation for those who embrace certain types of non-reductive physicalism (including emergence) is generated by "an attempt to combine 'upward determination' with 'downward causation.'" In his book *Physicalism or Something Near Enough* he presents an argument against mental causation that he calls the "supervenience/exclusion" argument. Kim's argument can be stated fairly simply once we understand the following four principles (some of which are already familiar to us):

(P1) *Supervenience:* "the claim that what happens in our mental life is wholly dependent on, and determined by, what happens in our bodily processes."[39]

(P2) "*The causal closure of the physical domain:* If a physical event has a cause at t, then it has a physical cause at t."[40]

(P3) "*Principle of causal exclusion:* If an event *e* has a sufficient cause *c* at *t*, no event at *t* distinct from *c* can be a cause of *e* (unless this is a genuine case of causal overdetermination)."[41]

(P4) *Mental/Physical property dualism:* "the view that mental properties are irreducible to physical properties."[42]

Here is how Kim's argument proceeds:[43]

1. M causes M*.

2. For some physical property P*; M* has P* as its supervenience base.

3. M causes M* by causing its physical supervenience base P*.

4. M is a cause of P*.

   By *Closure* it follows:

5. P* has a physical cause—call it P—occurring at the time M occurs.

39. Kim, *Physicalism, or Something near Enough*, 14.
40. Ibid., 15.
41. Ibid., 17.
42. Ibid., 22.
43. Ibid., 44. Kim offers two different "completions" of his argument. The following argument is what he refers to as "completion 2." See Kim, *Physicalism*, 39–44, for a rendering of both versions of the argument.

6. $M \neq P$ (by *Irreducibility*).

7. Hence, P* has two distinct causes, M and P, and this is not a case of causal overdetermination.

8. Hence, by *Exclusion*, either M or P must go.

9. By *Closure* and *Exclusion*, M must go; P stays.

It should be obvious how this argument applies to Clayton's version of strong emergence with his corresponding commitment to (SS) and (C). If all of Kim's principles are accepted, then, according to the "supervenience/exclusion" argument, all of the causal work is accomplished at the physical level leaving the mental as merely epiphenomenal and causally inert. We would now be left with the following picture.

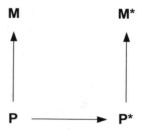

Of course, this picture would be unacceptable to Clayton, first because it denies mental causation outright, and second because it leaves no room for the ontological openness needed if divine activity is going to be allowed. On this picture, the problems that faced Clayton at the beginning regarding divine activity and causal closure would simply recur all over again.

But why should Clayton accept Kim's argument as it stands? One possible response open to him is to reject premise (7). He could do this by claiming that it is in fact illicit to state that M and P are actually two *distinct and independent* causes of P*. Barry Loewer states that rather than thinking of P and M as two distinct causes, like two assassins simultaneously hitting their victim (what Loewer calls independent overdetermination), we may think of them as a single metaphysically linked cause (what Loewer calls *dependent overdetermination*). Here is how dependent overdetermination works. Loewer asks us to imagine "a neurophysiological event N realizing a mental event M (say, a desire for a sip of beer) and where both cause E (say the subject's hand's moving)."[44] To match our diagrams above, we may refer to the neurophysiological event as P, the desire for a sip of beer as M, and the effect of moving the hand as P*. We may now talk about the link between P and M counterfactually by noting that M depends on P such that if P did not obtain, then neither would M. Furthermore, if P and M did not obtain, then neither would P*. We may also counterfactually state that the nature of the subvenient base P is such that any world in which P obtains is also a world that contains M.[45] In this case P and M are linked in such a way that they are not two distinct causes of P* but one metaphysically linked cause of P*. Now if Clayton's account of emergence is in fact true, then it may very well be the case that some type of "dependent overdetermination" is also true. Talking about emergence and mental causation in this way can solve various problems. First, if this scenario were true, then, as I mentioned, Clayton would be able to avoid any violation of Kim's *Exclusion* principle because P and M would be sufficiently linked so as to count as a single cause rather than two independent causes. Second, this possibility would also be able to explain correlationism, since it would be the case that emergent properties are metaphysically linked to their subvenient base such that it would be (metaphysically) natural for every mental state to have a corresponding physical state. Third, thinking of "P and M" as the jointly necessary and sufficient cause of P* would also amount to a rejection of Kim's closure principle since a non-physical (mental) cause would be necessary (though not sufficient) to bring about a physical state of affairs (something *closure* denies). However, this denial of *closure* is different than the simple dualist denial of closure since, on this account, the mental property is metaphysically (rather than contingently) linked to the physical subvenient base. In this case, there would never be a "free-floating" mental cause requiring an explanation. The linking together of P and M is also a fairly close rendering of the agent causation Clayton sometimes defends, and to which our discussion will briefly turn.

Clayton's version of agent causation is sometimes presented as a way to blend the phenomenological aspect of mental causation (or the "folk" aspect of mental causation) with the physical fact of correlationism. He writes that "[p]henomenology . . . provides a type of analysis that is com-

---

44. Loewer, "Review of "Mind in a Physical World, 318.
45. See for example, Block, "Do Causal Powers Drain Away?" 133–50.

mitted to providing data on mental causation without heavy imports of ontology."[46] Beginning with the phenomenological experience of mental causation (or "folk-causation"), Clayton then links the physical with the mental and refers to the whole as the *psycho-somatic* acting agent. He writes, "Humans are both body and mind, in the sense that we manifest both biological and mental causal features, and both in an interconnected manner. The mental characteristics depend on the physical, in a manner analogous to other dependency relations of emergent phenomena throughout the biosphere.[47] This account of agent causation is nothing but the *dependent overdetermination* account of causation suggested by Loewer and outlined above. On both accounts (i.e., agent causation and *dependent overdetermination*) mental and physical causes are epistemologically separable while being metaphysically linked. The final question is whether such an account leaves room for the ontological openness that Clayton desires.

Let us allow for the sake of argument that every non-dualistic account of mental causation involves both a mental predicate and a physical correlate. Let us further allow that while the mental is not identical (or reducible) to the physical, the two properties are metaphysically inseparable and jointly the cause of the new physical base. On this account there will never be a purely mental cause of any physical state of affairs although there will be "mental/physical" causes of some physical states of affairs. Now, this may be a way to allow something like mental causation into our ontology, but as far as Clayton is concerned this solution is no more acceptable than the emergent dualist solution offered above since it leads us back to our initial difficulty. The problem is that there is still a form of closure lurking around; this is, for better or worse, what a commitment to correlationism entails. It may be that the mental is causally "doing its own thing" and that the corresponding physical state is just an accidental trivial coincidence, but in that case we are back to mental causation being utterly mysterious. In trying to link emergence and mental causation with the natural sciences, Clayton has outlined a type of physicalism in which all the causal work is described at the level of the physical *even if there exists a metaphysically necessary mental cause as well*. If there is a physical correlate for every mental cause, then we may accept dependent

---

46. Clayton, *Mind and Emergence*, 140–41.
47. Ibid., 143. Emphasis in original.

overdetermination. However, this solution will not be sufficient to create the type of ontological openness that Clayton wants in order to show how divine action is possible. Going back to an earlier diagram will show why.

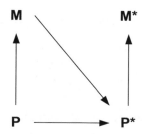

According to emergence theory, the emergence of M from P cannot be predicted or explained in advance; however, we can (at least in principle) tell the causal story *ex post facto*. That is, unless some sort of Malebranchian occasionalism is true (in which case emergence would be false), we can explain (after the fact) how the properties of the emergent base (and their relations) give rise to M. Let us call this causal story P1. Now what about the causal move from P to P*? It seems that we would be justified in believing that the causal exchange that occurs between P and P* could also be spelled out in purely physical terms. Let us call this explanation P2. Now since P2 is not sufficient alone to explain P*, we still need an account of the causal exchange between M and P*. However, there is no *physically* causal story to be told about M causing P* except to spell out P1 and P2. If we know how P causes M and P contributes to the cause of P*, then we know all there is to know *physically speaking*. As far as science is concerned, the causal story will move upward from P to M and horizontally from P to P*. This does not mean that M has no role to play. M is certainly important since M comes into existence when P does and P (physically with M) causes P*. However, there is no *scientifically interesting* story that can be told about M's causal powers outside of telling the causal story of P (and its causal effects both vertically and horizontally). So even on Clayton's non-dualist account of mental causation, he has not avoided the pitfalls of casual closure that plagued divine action in the first place. Even if God wanted to influence human behavior by influencing human mentality, God would still have to break into the causal chain moving from P to M or P to P*. So while the emergent dualist account of mental causation left an unpalatable breach in the nomological structure of the physical world thus alienating the sciences, the non-reductive physicalist account has recreated the problem of causal closure shutting God, once again, out of the world.

FREEDOM *FROM* GOD: A THEOLOGICAL EPILOGUE

It may be that the problem Clayton faces in relation to divine action and mental causation is similar to the problems that plagued Barbour and Dembski in the preceding chapters. Namely, in trying to delineate the meaning of a religious concept by looking to the natural sciences, Clayton is distorting religious meaning and showing himself to be an able practitioner of religious scientism. This, however, may not be the end of the story. Clayton's intellectual position isn't anything if not elusive, and in his latest book on the topic of human freedom, Clayton seems to be leaning towards taking theological meaning a bit more seriously. While Clayton's latest forage into human freedom may not create the ontological space needed for God's reentrance into the world, it does seem to be a bit more theologically satisfying. While a complete account of his most recent construal of human freedom is beyond the interest of this chapter, I do want to point out two important aspects of his view and see how they relate to the discussion of divine action outlined above.

In the last chapter of his book *In Quest of Freedom*, Clayton admits the failure of trying to derive any account of human freedom from the idea of emergence alone. He writes, "Working within the framework of natural emergence, we have not been able to establish that humans are free in the strongest sense; the possibility has remained that ascriptions of freedom are part of a regulative (and hence fictional) practice of self-interpretation regarding behaviors that are in fact causally determined."[48] While for some this philosophical dead-end may mark the end of a search for human freedom, Clayton perseveres, turning his sights to religious anthropology. Specifically, he attempts to make sense of the meaning of human freedom by looking in two different, but related, directions. First, he seeks to revisit the panentheistic analogy, this time using the language of *imago Dei*. Second, he attempts to make sense of human freedom by allowing for the possibility of what I call "teleological transcendence."

Both of Clayton's recent proposals for dealing with human freedom involve extending our ontological commitments beyond the natural

---

48. Clayton, *In Quest of Freedom*, 138.

world to include something like a transcendent spiritual reality. However, this spiritual reality is not utterly transcendent since Clayton remains a committed panentheist. Earlier we saw that Clayton hoped to use the panentheistic analogy as a way of explaining the relationship between human freedom and divine action. The goal was to show how free human mental acts could serve as a way of making sense of divine activity. In a reversal of the panentheistic analogy, Clayton, in *In Quest for Freedom*, flips the analogical argument on its head. Using the language of *imago Dei* (or the "image of God") correlations, Clayton now seeks to make sense of human freedom by appealing to the possibility that a panentheistic God can interact with (or in) the world. He writes, "Correlations between specific notions of God and specific interpretations of human freedom are a particular form of *imago Dei* correlations. The category of *imago Dei* correlations in which I will focus attempts to formulate analogies between God's relation to the world, on the one hand, and the relation of human persons to their bodies, and hence to the entire physical-casual order, on the other. In any given case the two side are not identical, of course; yet in any coherent system they should at least be analogous"[49] Clayton seems to want to argue that one way to understand human freedom is by first understanding the God-world relation. If such understanding could be accomplished, we could then point to the idea of a correlation between God's acts and ours to get a grip on how human acts could be free. Clayton writes, "I have suggested that the logic of the God-world relation offers a potentially fruitful way to approach the problem of human freedom, and indeed the question of the nature of the human agent in general."[50] The problem is that this same sort of analogy, as we have seen above, was supposed to be used to make sense of God's relation to the world. Putting Clayton's two uses of the panentheistic analogy together we get the following circle: We can understand God's action in the world analogically by making sense of human freedom, and we can understand human freedom in terms of understanding God's action in the world and then utilizing the concept of *imago Dei* correlations; however, we understand God's action in the world by understanding human freedom . . . (*circulus in probando*). We seemed to have lost our way by returning to the place where we started. We are still left wondering what exactly the God-world relation is supposed to amount to as well as continuing to be stymied about the question of human freedom.

49. Ibid. 139.
50. Ibid. 140–41.

Things fare no better when we attempt to solve the problem of human freedom with reference to the possibility of a human orientation towards divine transcendence. We can easily imagine human beings coming to a point where they subjectively transcend the extra mundane "stuff" of the world around them. In such instances, they come to think of their lives as both more than the sum total of physical facts and as a life lived under the purview of the divine. In fact, this is probably how many (or most) religious believers live. Clayton writes, "if a person's emergent capacity to transcend her given context and framework allows her to orient herself vis-à-vis a really existent transcendent being or dimension, then it may well give rise to a richer notion of freedom."[51] Of course, the question is how this is suppose to occur? How can the subjective orientation of a life toward *anything* give rise to ontologically real human freedom? As far as I can tell, the answer is found in our theological commitments. "According to the hypothesis in its theistic form, God's overarching goal is that, given the total set of constraining conditions, a complex enough organism should emerge that it becomes capable of raising the question of the ultimate meaning of human existence and of freely entering into a relationship with the ground of its existence."[52] However, despite Clayton's use of "hypothesis" his conclusion is theological in nature and not philosophical (or scientific). There is no argument, just an explanation of what human freedom means in the context of theological discourse. Yet, maybe this is enough.

While it is quite difficult to see how either of these accounts of human freedom adds anything to the philosophical or scientific discussion of the subject, I do think Clayton has made a valuable theological contribution to understanding human freedom by placing it in the context of the divine/human relationship. While a theological circle may not convince any but those already in the circle, it is a good way to garner conceptual clarity. Clayton may be preaching to the choir, but it is the same choir that has made up his audience from the beginning. Rather than trying to artificially expand the choir to encompass those who do not want to sing, Clayton may do well to simply recognize that his work is best taken as an extended sermon rather than a piece of philosophy. And there is nothing wrong with a good sermon.

51. Ibid., 144.
52. Ibid., 147.

5

Making Room for God in the World

A T THE BEGINNING OF the last chapter I indicated how a miracle could be taken, not as an odd event contrary to nature, but as a way of interpreting the religious significance of some (possibly mundane) event or another. This idea was seen in the story of the lady who saw the "weeping" statue of Mary as a revelation from God without any concern whatsoever for trying to explain what was happening. The same idea works in the other direction as well; an odd event does not immediately entail a miracle. I remember when I was an undergraduate student at the University of Washington, I once asked my Islam professor, for reasons I do not remember now, about the resurrection of Jesus. He related to me a story about a lecture he attended many years ago when he was a student at Harvard. The lecture was on the various forms of evidence that pointed to the high probability that Jesus died and came back to life again after being placed in a tomb. He told me that all this type of evidence would show, even if it was in fact true, was that some odd event occurred and someone came back from the dead. It was many years later that I read Simone Weil who wrote, "Hitler could die and return to life again fifty times, but I should not look upon him as the Son of God."[1] Weil and my professor were simply stating the obvious; namely, that there is nothing religiously interesting, in and of itself, about someone coming back to life after being dead (although scientifically this would be of great interest). What makes the odd event religiously significant—what makes it a resurrection—is not its oddity but its *context*. It was the life of Jesus and the experience his followers had when they were with him that made the resurrection something more than simply a zombie-like return to life. Odd events do

1. Weil, *Letters to a Priest*, 34. Quoted in Strandberg, *The Possibility of Discussion: Relativism, Truth and Criticism of Religious Beliefs*, 24.

not a miracle make any more than common events restrict the possibility of the miraculous; what is important is whether we can *see* God *in* an event or not.

It is quite natural for believers to see God "in" various places and "in" various things scattered throughout the world. Some say that God lives *in* their hearts, or that God is *in* the beauty of the mountains. Others see God manifest *in* the birth of their child, *in* the beauty that is often present in a peaceful death, *in* the consecrated Eucharist, or even *in* the statue of a saint that appears to be weeping. Of course, someone may respond that God is not actually "in" any of those things; it is just that when some individuals are in the presence of certain states of affairs they are reminded of God (or possibly begin to think about God). Subsequently, we may feel that the believer is misusing language in a way that needs to be corrected. The oddity is that the religious sense of "in" already has a perfectly sensible use. This use makes sense because we realize that when we say God is "in" something we are generally aware that God is not an object among objects that exists in things in the same way that two physical objects can be in one another. Certainly God is not in my heart in the way that the dog is in the car or the beans are in the Chili. When we speak of God being "in" something we pay attention to what is being said so as not to make the mistake of misconstruing the meaning of the religious individuals confession of faith (I take it that "In the Beginning . . ." is not a temporal statement either).

It isn't only the religious uses of "in" that require us to pay attention to the meaning of the word in order to ascertain what is being said. It is because we have some grasp of the diversity of meanings that "in" possesses that we are not compelled to send out a search party when someone says the "devil is in the details" or sift through our dessert when we hear that the "proof of the pudding is in the eating." It is only when we lose sight of the sense (or use) of "in" that we feel compelled to think we have discovered an instance of nonsense.

There is something akin to semantic spiritual blindness at work when Arthur Peacocke, writing about God's interaction with the world, tries to make sense of what it means to say God is "in" the world by looking to the natural sciences. The problem, as we shall see, isn't that Peacocke sees God at work in the world (what believer doesn't?), but rather that he turns away from religion in order to explain what this type of "seeing" means. Much like Clayton in the last chapter, the sense of what Peacocke has to say depends on the specifics of his argument. However, *contra* Clayton's argument for mental causation, Peacocke's argument—being that it is free of any actual empirical claims that can be falsified—may be able to be interpreted as a religiously significant way of seeing God in the world. In this chapter I want to present a summary explanation of Peacocke's panentheism, showing why I believe such an account of the God/world relation falls short. I will conclude by pointing out a new way to interpret Peacocke's claims that make his argument religiously worthwhile.

BETWEEN PANTHEISM AND CLASSICAL THEISM

As I mentioned in the last chapter, panentheism is etymologically the view that all (*pan*) is in (*en*) God (*theism*), but God is more than (or transcends) the totality of finite things. A bit more poetically, the *Oxford Dictionary of the Christian Church* defines panentheism as "The belief that the being of God includes and penetrates the whole universe, so that every part of it exists in him, (as against Pantheism) that His being is more than, and is not exhausted by, the universe."[2] Panentheism, as seen in this definition, is a way to maintain God's immanence without identifying God with the world. Just as importantly, however, panentheism is also a way of retrieving divine immanence from a theistic conception of the God/world relation that separates God and creation so radically that the only way for God to enter "into" the world is through a divine interruptive miracle, the kind that Clayton found so problematic. This radical separation of God from the world is generally referred to as classical theism, which, as Peacocke writes, "conceived of God as a necessary 'substance' with attributes and posited a space 'outside' God in which the realm of the created was located—for one entity cannot exist in another and retain its own (ontological) identity when they are regarded as substances."[3] So while panentheism is indeed a way of avoiding the perils of pantheism, it is also a way of dealing with the travesty of utter transcendence.

As a *via media* between these two extremes, panentheism can also be seen as a way of maintaining the best attributes of pantheism and classical theism without being committed to the negative aspects of these ways of

---

2. Cross and Livingstone, *The Oxford Dictionary of the Christian Church*, 1027. Quoted in Peacocke, *In Whom We Live*, xviii.

3. Peacocke, "Articulating God's Presence," 145.

thinking about the God world relation. For instance, panentheism hopes to find a place for God within the structure of nature by placing nature in God. In this sense, to think of the world being "in" God does not have the same meaning as God being "in" the world, since the latter (but not the former) can be (but need not be) taken as a way of saying that God and the world are, strictly speaking, identical. That is, if God is taken as being in the world, period, then there is no place outside the world were God is (this is pantheism); however, since for the panentheist the world is in God, there is no place where the world exists that is outside of God. By reversing the position of the terms that flank the preposition "in" ("world in God" rather than "God in the world"), panentheism has created a way of talking about God that stresses the immanence of pantheism while also maintaining the transcendence of God emphasized in classical theism.

With this general outline of the goals of panentheism in mind, it should be noted that there is a specific difficulty facing anyone trying to write on the topic; namely, panentheism is more a family of related ideas rather than one simple, easy-to-define concept. Part of the problem is that panentheism is usually packaged as a component of a wider philosophical or theological system, which then explains panentheism using its own unique jargon and philosophical terminology. This intermingling of theological panentheism with philosophy and philosophical theology is seen clearly in John Cooper's recent critical survey of panentheism that place individuals as diverse as Jonathan Edwards, Samuel Taylor Coleridge, and James Cone all under the banner of panentheists.[4] Recently, however, panentheism has enjoyed a bit of streamlined popularity becoming the favored theological position of many of those who write in the area of science and religion. My focus in this chapter is on one voice in the plethora of panentheistic voices represented under the heading that John Cooper refers to as "Panentheism in Theological Cosmology"; namely, the voice of the late scientist/theologian Arthur Peacocke. It is to his particular panentheism that we now turn.

PEACOCKE'S PANENTHEISM: NATURE AS EXPLANANDUM, GOD AS EXPLANANS

Peacocke believes that the contemporary view of the natural world offered by science impresses upon us a need to develop a new way to look at the

---

4. See, Cooper, *Panentheism*, 301–18.

relationship between God and the world. He writes, "Many developments in science itself have led to a radical transformation of that [Newton/Boyle] mechanical picture of the natural world; these in turn have led to a profound reconsideration by Christian theists (and others) of how, in the light of the sciences, to conceive of God's relation to the world as it is now perceived to be and to be becoming."[5] In order to understand why such a reformation is necessary, it is essential to take a look at how science, according to Peacocke, currently views the natural world.

Peacocke begins his explanation of panentheism by looking at two different, but related, ways of looking at the natural world described by contemporary science. He refers to these as the "synchronic" view and the "diachronic" view. As the labels suggest, the synchronic view is a sort of frozen-in-time snapshot of the natural world that pays particularly close attention to the variety of emergent levels that exist in the natural world. The diachronic view, on the other hand, focuses on the evolutionary process that has occurred through time with particular attention given to the way that the world is able to create novel entities and structures within a naturalistic (non-interventionist) framework. Since both of these ways of looking at the world are important to Peacocke's overall account of panentheism, we will look at each in turn.

Peacocke's synchronic view is a fairly straightforward account of the multi-layered view of reality expressed by the contemporary science of emergence and presented in the last chapter. Peacocke explains the core of the synchronic view when he writes, "The natural (and human) sciences more and more give us a picture of the world as consisting of complex hierarchies—a series of levels of organizations of matter in which each successive member is a whole constituted of parts preceding it in the series."[6] On the whole, Peacocke's emergence has much in common with the emergence of Philip Clayton outlined in the last chapter. For example, Peacocke takes emergent properties to be properties that are novel, irreducible and (oftentimes) causally efficacious. He also thinks of the mind as an emergent property dependent on the body but not identical to it. A person, for Peacocke, is best seen as "psychosomatic unities with physical, mental and spiritual capacities."[7] There is, however, one glaring

5. Peacocke, "Articulating God's Presence," 137.

6. Ibid., 138.

7. Ibid., 140.

and important difference between Clayton and Peacocke that should be mentioned, namely, what each means when they refer to their respective positions as "monistic."

To call yourself a "monist" is simply to claim that you believe that all is "one." Of course, the difficulty is in spelling out what is meant by "one." This difficulty was one of the main projects for the early Greek pre-Socratic philosophers. Thales thought that the "one" was water, Anaximenes took it to be air, and Heraclitus thought of it as the fact that everything is subject to change. Clayton's monism is comprised of the claim that all of reality is composed of the same "stuff," and, whatever this "stuff" is, it is not identical with the types of things described by physics. Clayton writes, "Reality is ultimately composed of one basic kind of stuff. Yet the concepts of physics *are not* sufficient to explain all the forms that this stuff takes . . . The one 'stuff' apparently takes forms for which the explanations of physics, and thus the ontology of physics . . . *are not* adequate. We should not assume that the entities postulated by physics complete the inventory of what exists. Hence the emergentists should be monists but not physicalists."[8] In this case, the one stuff is defined by the fact that it is *whatever* all things are composed of.

While Clayton's monism may seem a bit *ad hoc*, it is not without historical precedent. The Greek pre-Socratic philosopher Anaximander thought of the "one" as the undefined *apeiron* (or "infinite") that is responsible for bringing into being (with the help of motion) all that exists. It should also be noted that while Clayton's ontology of "stuff" is not, strictly speaking, physicalist, it is meant to be parsimonious. However, since his ontology includes at least the material objects that describes plus the "stuff" itself of which these objects (and everything else) are composed, his ambiguous parsimony may tend to bloat his ontology.

Like Clayton, Peacocke also considers himself a monist; however, *contra* Clayton, he takes everything to be ultimately constituted by the fundamental particles described by physics. His "one" is that which we learn about in physics class; all the rest is constituted by (or emerges from) this physical "stuff." He, therefore, refers to his type of monism as "emergent monism." This does not mean that the entities that are constituted by physical particles and their relations are not real, but it does mean that all things that exist "can be broken down into fundamental physical

8. Clayton, *Mind and Emergence*, 4. Emphasis added.

entities and that no extra entities are thought to be inserted at higher levels of complexity to account for their properties."[9] This makes Peacocke's emergent monism a species of physicalism (or what Peacocke might call "naturalism"). Peacocke writes, "I shall presume at least this with the 'physicalist': all concrete particulars in the world (including human beings)—with all of their properties—are constituted only of fundamental physical entities of matter/energy at the lowest level and manifested in many layers of complexity."[10]

The distinction between Peacocke's "emergent monism" and Clayton's "monism" should not cloud the similarities that both share with regard to the synchronic picture of reality. They are both dyed in the wool emergentists who stress the multi-leveled variety that exists in the natural world. The synchronic view is simply a time-slice of the natural world that stresses emergent levels as interconnected and interdependent while also stressing how this process is possible without any supernatural tinkering.

Of course, the emergence represented by the synchronic view is a bit of a *chimera* since it is cut off from the processes that make such emergence possible. This lacunae, however, is ameliorated by Peacocke with the presentation of what he calls the "diachronic" view. The diachronic explanation, as the title suggests, is an attempt to represent the emergence described in the synchronic view as a process that has occurred over long periods of time. Peacocke refers to this process as the "epic of evolution" (using "epic" I imagine, to suggest something dynamic, creative and temporally expansive). Peacocke contrasts the creative/active "epic of evolution" with the more static/mechanistic position developed by Isaac Newton. More than a simple retelling of the familiar story of evolution, however, Peacocke's "epic" story attempts to point out certain salient features of the diachronic process that are especially relevant for guiding us in developing our reformed view of divine action.

The first, and I think most important, aspect of the diachronic view is Peacocke's commitment to causal closure; or, the claim that all of the causal exchanges that occur (and have occurred) in the history of the evolutionary process can be explained in purely naturalistic terms. Peacocke writes, "The nexus of causality is unbroken and now requires no *deus ex machina*, no 'God of the gaps,' to explain *inter alia* the cosmic develop-

---

9. Peacocke, "Articulating God's Presence," 139.

10. Peacocke, *All That Is*, 12.

ment, the formation of planet earth, the transition from inorganic to living matter, the origin of species, and the development of complex brains that have the capacity to be aware."[11] The commitment to causal closure is also evident when Peacocke writes that "[A] notable aspect of the scientific account of the natural world in general is the seamless character of the web that has been spun on the loom of time; at no point do modern natural scientists have to invoke any non-natural causes to explain their observations and inferences about the past."[12] Closure, on this account, means that the "epic of evolution," being the process that led to the emergence of more complex life forms, is also a process whose occurrence is fully explainable in terms of the natural sciences. It isn't that the scientist is only telling part of the story; rather, the account is either fully complete or simply in need of a more complete causal account.

For Peacocke, causal closure is only one side of the diachronic coin. Equally important is the way that this closed causal system is able— through the process of complex systems self-organizing—to give rise to the types of emergent realties outlined above. Peacocke writes, "Although the second law of thermodynamics entails an exorable overall increase in entropy (and so of randomness and disorder) in the universe as a whole, it is now understood, in terms of both irreversible and stochastic kinetics, how new complex structures can arise even within homogeneous physicochemical systems, especially when they involve a flux of matter and / or energy.[13] The interesting feature of the diachronic process is the way that the novel entities of emergence arise out of the creative interaction of natural laws acting on complex systems. Peacocke's foil, once again, is the mechanistic view described by Isaac Newton (and later taken up by his deist successors). The heart of this juxtaposition seems to be a scientific view of nature that statically progresses, like a row of geese flying south for the Winter that periodically adds and subtracts a goose at various intervals in a law like manner, and nature that is in a constant state of stochastic change, like a swarm of bees whose constant interaction creates a series of varying novel patterns over time. It isn't that the geese are not progressing; they do make it south after all, but what is missing is the creative novelty that complex systems often develop when they are worked

11. Peacocke, "Articulating God's Presence", 141.

12. Peacocke, *All That Is*, 19.

13. Peacocke, "Articulating God's Presence," 141.

upon by natural laws. Peacocke writes, "The processes of the world by their inherent properties manifest a spontaneous creativity in which new properties emerge."[14] It is this progressive naturalistic creativity that lies at the heart of the diachronic view of nature.

GOD'S ACTS AND NATURE'S CAUSES

It is in the context of the current scientific view of the world just outlined that Peacocke believes any account of divine action must take place. In fact, according to Peacocke, it is by utilizing and working within the scientific view of nature that theologians come to take science seriously. The goal, at least for Peacocke, is to develop a theological account of the God/world relation that takes the synchronic and diachronic view seriously. Of course, in placing the meaning of divine action at the mercy of our current science, certain possibilities are immediately ruled out. For instance, since Peacocke sees the world of science as causally closed, he rules out the type of solution offered by Clayton in the last chapter; a view that called for ontological openness and the denial of closure. Furthermore, while Peacocke doesn't appear to think that a divine interruption of the causal order is impossible, he does seem to think it is a possibility that has dwindled as our scientific knowledge of causal exchanges has increased.[15] What is needed is a way of talking about Divine action that sees God's creativity as being one with the causal accounts that are explained by our best science. Peacocke writes, "God *must* now be seen as creating in the world, often through what science calls 'chance' operating within the created order, each stage of which constitutes the launching pad for the next."[16] Panentheism offers Peacocke just what he needs. By placing nature within God, we get, by fiat, a way of seeing everything that occurs in the world as a part of the Divine nature. In what follows I want to look at Peacocke's account of Divine action as it relates to both causal closure and to his panentheism.

So what does it mean, according to Peacocke, to say that God has acted? As we already saw, Peacocke appears to be content to talk about divine action as a set of events that are co-extensive with the causal processes that science describes. Take the following quotes as evidence:

14. Ibid., 142.

15. See, Peacocke, *Paths from Science*, chapter 5.

16. Peacocke, "Articulating God's Presence," 143. Emphasis added.

1. "We have to emphasize anew the immanence of God as creator 'in, with, and under' the natural processes of the world unveiled by the sciences in accord with all the sciences have revealed since those debates in the nineteenth century"[17]

2. "a *theistic* naturalism may be expounded according to which natural processes, characterized by the laws and regularities discovered by the natural sciences, are themselves actions of God, who continuously gives them existence."[18]

3. "The work of God as Creator is regarded as manifest in all the time in those very natural processes that are unveiled by the sciences in all their regularities."[19]

All these quotes show that for Peacocke the actions of God are best seen in the various instances of causal regularities described by the various sciences. But why call these causal exchanges divine acts? What is the actual role that God plays in such a naturalistic account of the world? Is God a necessary condition, a sufficient condition, or jointly necessary and sufficient? All of these are important questions that I can only begin to answer.

One way to think about divine action is counterfactually. That is, we may say that if the causal interactions described by science were not also divine actions, then we would not have the type of world we in fact have. In this case Divine actions are seen as causes that actually make a difference. While much of Peacocke's discussion of divine action avoids any direct claim that the world is the way it is because of God's intervening acts, he does point in this direction when he writes, "God is the immanent creator creating through the processes of the natural order. The processes are not themselves God, but the *action* of God as creator."[20] That this Divine act is supposed to be a cause that makes a difference is seen when Peacocke writes, "God is creating at every moment of the world's existence through perpetually giving creativity to the very stuff of the world."[21] This makes it appear that Peacocke wants to say that in each causal exchange described by science there is both a natural process and

17. Peacocke, "Articulating God's Presence," 143.
18. Peacocke, *All That Is*, 17. Emphasis in original.
19. Ibid., 9.
20. Peacocke, "Articulating God's Presence," 144. Emphasis in original.
21. Ibid.

a divine process described in naturalistic language. So while scientists think they are simply describing naturalistic causal laws, they are actually, unbeknownst to many of them, describing acts of divine creation. This, however, is a mistake, and in order to understand why we need to turn back, once again, to panentheism.

If panentheism is correct and the world is in God, then there must exist a certain ontological closeness between natural causes and God's creative acts. In fact, this closeness would be such that the causal exchanges described by science would actually *be* instances of divine action. Peacocke writes, "For God is best conceived of as the circumambient Reality enclosing all existing entities, structures, and processes and as operating in and through all, while being more than all. Hence all that is not God has its existence within God's operation and being. . . . God creates all-that-is within Godself while remaining ontologically distinct."[22] The causal exchanges described by science are co-extensive with the creative acts of God because nature is co-extensive with an aspect of the Divine nature. It isn't that there are causal laws *and* the acts of God, rather there are the causal laws that, being part of God, are part of God's creative acts. The panentheistic solution gets Divine actions on the cheap once they place the world within God. Panentheism is an attempt to take causal closure seriously while also creating a place for God's acts that can a) operate within the bounds of the constraint created by closure, and b) be taken as a cause that makes a difference when it comes to explaining the emergence and creativity that is seen in the contemporary scientific description of the natural world.

While this seems to be a logical way to talk about divine action, one gets the feeling of being cheated similar to the way that the ontological argument cheats us when it proves the logical impossibility of denying God's existence. Now since Peacocke has not so much argued for Divine action as much as he has simply explained what he means by the concept, what follows are not knock-down arguments against panentheism, but rather a set of loosely related criticisms meant to show that Peacocke's panentheism is inadequate as a general project for relating science and religion. However, I will close by also gesturing towards some of the ways that I think Peacocke's panentheism succeeds in offering a theologi-

22. Ibid., 146.

cally sufficient account of how the believer may view science *sub specie aeternitatis*.

EMERGENT MONISM AND CAUSAL POWERS

Before looking at specific conceptual and theological problems that haunt Peacocke's panentheism, I want to point to a philosophical problem that at least calls for further clarification. Peacocke seems to be committed to something akin to an inconsistent triad. Take the following three statements:

1. There are no non-natural causes.

2. While there are real emergent levels, these levels are all constituted by properties and relations that are describable in the language of contemporary science.

3. Emergent levels are (sometimes) causally efficacious.

We are now left with the task of trying to make sense of (3) in light of (1) and (2). Here is the problem. If an emergent level is going to be causally efficacious and ontologically real, then the causal exchange that occurs must be an exchange that can be described in the language of the natural sciences (specifically physics). When we think of emergent systems that are themselves physical, we seem to have no problem because the new emergent physical system can produce "new" causal powers that are still themselves physical (and, hence, describable in the language of physics). However, what about emergent properties that are novel and irreducible yet not physical? We have seen how Peacocke's view of constitution can account for such properties; these putative non-physical emergent properties are constituted by the physical base from which they emerge. So far so good, however, what about the causal powers of the non-physical emergent properties, for example, the mind? Peacocke can either say that the mental exhibits causal powers not describable in the language of physics, or he can bite the bullet and say that all the causal work is done at the physical level. The former solution is unintelligible since the mental *qua* mental cannot interact in the type of purely physical causal exchanges that Peacocke desires; however, the latter solution makes mental properties epiphenomenal. But this may not be the worst of it. There are hints that Peacocke's position may lead to a denial of the very properties that make human persons unique, namely, our conscious mental states.

There are times when Peacocke seems to equate ontological reality with causal powers. He writes that "[r]eal entities have influence and play irreducible roles in adequate explanations of the world"[23] He also states "[r]eal entities have effects and play irreducible roles in adequate explanations of the world."[24] We are now left not only wondering about the causal efficacy of the mental but also about its very reality. If mental properties are not causally efficacious, then there is a sense in which Peacocke seems to think they are unreal. While epiphenomenalism may deny that the mental has any causal powers, it does not deny its existence. What Peacocke offers is a view of human mentality that must be either reductionistic or eliminative; options that I take it Peacocke would find philosophically and theologically unsatisfying.

EVIL AND PANENTHEISM

In a telling passage from *All That Is*, Peacocke writes, "The processes [of the natural order] are not themselves God but are the *action* of God-as-creator—rather in the way that the processes and actions of our bodies as psychosomatic persons express ourselves."[25] In attaching divine action directly to the causal exchanges described by the sciences, Peacocke has indicted God as the cause of pain and suffering. Even worse, Peacocke seems to think that the types of causal exchanges that bring pain and suffering to the innocent are the *direct result* of God's intentions. When I bring about the causal act of getting off the couch, I do so because I intend to get an ice tea from the refrigerator. I, in my actions, express my intentions. Peacocke, in calling the processes of the natural order an action of God as creator, seems to imply that causal exchanges that lead to suffering and death are as much a part of God's creative actions as are the causal exchanges that lead to emergent creativity. This is what results when he attempts to link divine action with human mental acts.

Of course Peacocke is not unaware of the problem of evil. He even takes the fact that evil is contained "in" God to be a benefit of panentheism. He writes,

> Hence, when faced with this ubiquity of pain, suffering and death
> in the evolution of the living world, one is impelled to infer that

23. Peacocke, *All That Is*, 16.
24. Peacocke, "Articulating God's Presence," 139.
25. Peacocke, *All That Is*, 19. Emphasis in original.

> God, to be anything like the God who is love in Christian belief, must be understood to be suffering in the creative process of the world. . . . Now, when the natural world, with all its suffering, is panentheistically conceived of as "in God," it follows that the evils of pain, suffering, and death, in the world are internal to God's own self: God must have experience of the natural.[26]

The scare quotes that Peacocke places around "in God" represent the heart of the problem. First, what exactly does it mean that God *experiences* evil, pain, and suffering? Certainly, as most of us know, pain and suffering are things that are felt by finite human beings with sense organs and the ability to feel pain (both physical and emotional), yet, it is nonsense to state that these are experiences that God has (or can have) in any analogous way. God doesn't have a spinal cord, nervous system, or brain. God simply is not the type of entity that can have experiences *like* mine. Second, what is supposed to bring it about that the panentheistic God can now experience these things in a way God could not when God was thought of as being "outside" of (or transcendent over) creation? Did the experience come by means of proximity; that is, did God's physical (or ontological) closeness to pain, suffering, and death somehow give God the ability to existentially experience these things? Lastly, how does God's experience of such things (if we could make sense of this claim) make the state of affairs any better? Does God obtain new knowledge when God experiences pain such that God realizes that gratuitous suffering is not as good as once thought? Does God finally come to see how bad cancer in a child can be, thereby radically changing the course of nature? Or, maybe God is in the midst of a covert operation whereby nature has been infiltrated and is being changed from the inside out. This latter suggestion appears to be what Peacocke has in mind when he writes, "In a more specifically Christian perception, God in taking the suffering into God's own self can thereby transform it into what is whole and healthy—that is, be the means of 'salvation' when this is given its root etymological meaning. God heals and transforms from within as a healthy body might be regarded as doing."[27] But what does this healing amount to? Peacocke makes it appear as if there are some causal exchanges that are "good" that represent God's actions and intentions, while the "bad" causal exchanges, which lead to suffering and death, represent a sickness that God is trying

26. Peacocke, "Articulating God's Presence," 151.
27. Ibid., 152.

to heal. But Peacocke takes all causal exchanges—good, bad, and indiffer-ent—to be instances of divine action. Is God trying to heal with God's left hand what God is destroying with the right hand? Maybe all we can hope for is that God is left-handed.

ON GOD AND THINGS

We saw above that much of Peacocke's difficulty regarding divine action arises from his claim that classical theism, with its utterly transcendent God, represents a refusal to take contemporary science seriously. The problem, as Peacocke saw it, was that classical theism "conceived of God as a necessary 'substance' with attributes and posited a space 'outside' God in which the realm of the created was located—for one entity cannot exist in another and retain its own (ontological) identity when they are regard-ed as substances."[28] Yet, Peacocke seems to render terms such as "inside," "outside," and "substance" as if they were physical (or pseudo-physical) concepts rather than concepts with a perfectly clear religious sense.

What does Peacocke have in mind when he states that classical the-ism thinks of God as a substance situated "outside" the world? Is the out-side meant to be a spatial distance that separates God from creation? Are there borders in classical theism, like the borders that separate the United States from Canada, which separate God from the world? Even to sim-ply state that God is ontologically "outside" of creation tells us very little about what is meant by the one who utters such words. R. W. Hepburn brings out the oddity of attempting to apply univocal spatial predicates to God and objects when he writes, "[C]ompare these sentences—'Outside my room a sparrow is chirping,' 'Outside the city the speed limit ends,' 'Outside the earth's atmosphere meteors do not burn out,' and finally 'God is outside the universe, outside space and time.'"[29] In the first three cases, outside is used univocally. That is, it is used to denote physical things that stand in a certain spatial relationship to other physical things; but while there may be a *religious* sense of speaking of God as being "outside" the universe, this should not be taken as analogous to speaking of the loca-tion of one physical object in relation to others. If I said God is outside the universe in the way that the bird is outside my window, I am simply

28. Ibid., 145.

29. Hepburn, *Christianity and Paradox*. Quoted in D.Z. Phillips, *The Problem of Evil*. 164.

revealing my ignorance of theology and/or ornithology. Peacocke is mistaking a religious use of "outside" for a spatial use of the concept. His desire to move God from outside of the universe to inside the universe is motivated by thinking that such a move makes sense, yet this only makes sense on an erroneous construal of the meaning of "outside." Such an error, however, is parasitic on the spatial use of "outside" actually making sense when applied to God. However, it is possible that when classical theists speak of God as being "outside" they are simply expressing a religious truth about transcendence. It seems that a misunderstanding of classical theism's use of "outside" motivates Peacocke's panentheism; he appears to have dismantled a straw man of his own making.

What about Peacocke's use of "inside"? Is the world in God like the bread is in the breadbox? Niels Henrik Gregersen writes, "There may be as many panentheisms as there are ways of qualifying the world's being 'in God.'"[30] The problem, however, is not with the meaning of "in" in general, but with attempts to impose a univocal meaning of "in" onto two very different contexts. When Peacocke attempts to make sense of divine action by talking about the world being "in" God, he writes as if he needs to locate a place were we can find *evidence* of such "in-ness." This leads Peacocke to talk about the co-extensive nature of causal exchanges and divine creativity. The logic seems to be something like the following: When something is *in* something else there are always telltale signs of such "in-ness." To say that x is *in* y, and to also say that there is no physical evidence for x's being in y, is to simply say that x is *not* in y (remember John Wisdom's garden parable?). In broad strokes, I think this logic is correct. To say "Jesus lives in her heart" is to say that she (whoever she is) lives a certain way, acts a certain way, and treats others a certain way. There is indeed evidence for the fact that "Jesus lives in her heart." The mistake is to think that there are two states of affairs, namely, Jesus living in her heart *and* her living a certain way. In fact, what we really have is the fact that what we mean by "Jesus lives in her heart" is the fact that she lives a certain way. *We interpret her life as a life lived with Jesus in her heart.* The truth of the proposition is the same as the life that the woman lives. This distinction can, I think, help make sense of Peacocke's panentheism. Let me explain a bit further.

---

30. Gregersen, "Three Varieties," 19.

When Peacocke seeks to explain divine action in a way that makes the fact of God's being in the world co-extensive with the causal exchanges of science, he runs the risk of making Divine action superfluous. If "x causing y" is explicable in the language of physical causation, what room is left for the divine? What does the divine do? It appears that Peacocke wants us to believe that two *things* are present in any causal exchange. First, there is the naturalistic causal exchange described by physics, and second there is the divine action described by the theologian. But this isn't the only way to read these events. It may be that what we actually have is one event interpreted in two different (but For the believer God is in the world compatible) ways. What Peacocke may mean by God's presence in the world is simply that we interpret natural causal exchanges *as if* they were the acts of God. In this case the religious believer would look at the same facts that the atheist scientist sees while interpreting the selfsame facts in a vastly different manner. For the believer God is in the world acting through the causal exchanges, for the atheist the causal exchanges are all that there is. The believer does not add anything to the atheists account, it is simply that what the believer means by divine action is what the atheist scientist means by a scientific causal exchange. The believer would not deny the scientific causal account; they would simply interpret such an account as the acts of God. In this case the *en* (in) of pan*en*theism is simply the imposition of a religious interpretation onto the facts of science. No new facts, just new ways of seeing old facts. Of course, this view would not be of much interest to those who seek a "robust" account of the interaction between science and religion, and since Peacocke sets out to offer an account of divine action that takes science seriously, this lack of robustness should be made more explicit.

Let's assume that God's causal exchanges are sufficiently (though not exhaustively) described in terms of the causal language used by the natural sciences. We can accept that the causal language spoken by the scientist is actually an accurate description of how God creates such that the theologian can, in all sincerity, take such accounts as references to divine action. Where does this leave us as far as the relationship between science and religion goes? I think the answer is nowhere. There is no empirical sense that can be given to the claim that science is describing divine action, nor is there any scientific sense that can be given to the counterfactual claim that if God did not act in such and such a way, the world would not be as it is. Furthermore, there is nothing that a scientist has to learn in order to describe Divine creative acts, although there will be much that the theologian will have to learn about science in order to accurately describe what God is doing. At best, panentheism gives us causal overdetermination, since every causal exchange can be described in terms of physics and divine action. Science can continue to do its work providing an account of divine action without ever referring to a divine agent, but this means that science can simply go on as it always has. On this account, the contribution that Peacocke has made to science and religion is to show how divine action is a form of *interpreting* causal laws as if they were divine, but this doesn't seem to be the type of robustness that would seem interesting to those reading *Zygon* or winning Templeton prize money. However, maybe this reformed Peacockian position should receive more attention; in fact, I would argue that it is actually an interesting way to explain what the believer has in mind when they see God in the world (and isn't this what Peacocke was after all along?). Once we strip Peacocke's panentheism of its pseudo-scientific language and its practice of religious scientism we are actually left with a beautiful account of what believers may have in mind when they confess to seeing God in the world. In fact, I would argue that once we do the work of prying the scientific barnacles off of the sides of Peacocke's panentheism, what is left is an account of divine action that is semantically equivalent to the author of Genesis writing "In the beginning God . . ." (Gen 1:1). Maybe the best way to explain what I take to be the best part of Peacocke's panentheism is by ending with a biblical-like parable. Here is my first, and last, foray into storytelling.

LEARNING TO ENJOY INVISIBLE MAGIC

Using science to locate God in the world is a little like the magician who tried to make a career out of pulling an invisible rabbit out of a hat. He may have succeeded with each attempt, but nobody really knew for sure. In a similar way, maybe God is in the causal exchanges of science, but, even on Peacocke's construal, no one knows for sure. But this is not the only way to take Peacocke's suggestions.

Let's take the bit about the magician with the invisible rabbit a little further. Say the battle lines about the magician get drawn around those who say that the magician is deceived because there is no rabbit present, and those who say that there really is a rabbit present, albeit an invisible one. Just so this is not too much of a riddle, the former group are atheists who discount Peacocke's panentheism, and the latter group are those of Peacocke's ilk. Now, let us imagine a third group of people who are raised up in the tradition of "invisible magic." They have spent hours as children gathered around the fireplace while family members took turns playing the role of the magician with invisible props. They learned to appreciate the nuances of invisible magic, laughing at the funny gestures the magician makes and learning the difference between the end of a trick and merely a steppingstone to the grand finale. They have learned to read the magicians face and interpret the magicians moves. When the magician pulls the invisible rabbit out of the hat they roar with delight, applauding and asking for more. They understand the performance of the invisible magic show, they have played the game and know its nuances.

Now imagine that those who have been trained to appreciate invisible magic stumble across a debate between those who think the magician is a fraud and those who think that there is a real, albeit invisible, rabbit involved in the hat trick. These individuals are perplexed as they try to tell the debaters that the point isn't whether the rabbit is real or not. They even try to get both sides to see that the rabbit only has meaning in relation to the entire spectacle that is invisible magic. The debaters, however, brush them off as simpletons who simply are not bright enough to see the vital importance of settling the question of the ontological status of the rabbit. As the debate rages on, the simple folk run off to enjoy another evening of the context of the magic show. Maybe at some point, through the laughter and love, they take pity on the debaters, not so much because they are not enjoying the show, but more because they do not even see that the debate they have entered into with such gusto actually lacks any sense. By separating the question of the ontological status of the rabbit from the language game of invisible magic the debaters have mistaken a conceptual problem for an empirical one.

6

Taking A Religious Stance

IN HIS EPIC POEM *The Rime of the Ancient Mariner*, Samuel Taylor Coleridge has a salty weatherworn sailor recount the story of his high seas adventure to a somewhat frightened and disinterested wedding guest. The Mariner tells how his ship, pushed by a violent weather storm, ends up in a sea of ice enveloped in a blanket of fog. In the midst of this treachery, a somewhat playful and affable Albatross appears. The Albatross, seen as a good luck charm of sorts, leads the ship through a sudden opening that appears in the carpet of crackling ice. Then for some unknown reason, save for the possibility of breaking the boredom that must come from being stuck on a ship that is itself stuck at sea, the Mariner shoots the genial bird dead.

After the cruel and gratuitous killing of the Albatross, the ship finds itself drifting in searing heat on a still sea with no breeze to push it forward towards its destination. The crew, though surrounded by water, has no water to moisten their parched, dry mouths. With the growing consensus that their present suffering is related to the Mariner's murder of the Albatross, the crew fixes his penance. He is to carry the carcass of the dead Albatross around his neck. In the midst of the crews suffering, the Mariner spots a sign of hope, the faint silhouette of a ship. The hope of rescue is soon dashed as the welcome sight of the ship turns out to be a group of ghoulish skeleton-like seafarers who are playing a game of dice as a way of deciding the order in which the sailors will die. One-by-one, as the die is cast, the sailors drop dead peppering the deck of the ship with their carcasses. The hapless Mariner, spared to live a life surrounded by his dead shipmates and trapped with his own suffering, loneliness, and guilt, finds himself unable to utter even a word of prayer.

Then, something almost mystical happens to the grizzled old Mariner. In the midst of his thirst and discomfort, he undergoes a change. He begins to see his surroundings, including the slimy snakes that inhabit the sea, in a new way. Here is how J. R. Jones in his essay "Love as Perception of Meaning" explains what happened to the Mariner, "Then in the silence under the baking sun he began to look at what had earlier simply been an added loathsomeness—the slimy things which infested the water round the ship, and he began to be *aware* of them."[1] Awareness, however, is ambiguous. The Mariner's awareness took on a particular form. Jones continues, "His perception took on a timeless quality. The swarming water-snakes suddenly seemed to lie there with the whole world—the whole of existence—as their background. And this meant seeing them as they might be seen from Eternity. Something then welled up within him to which he could only give the name 'love' and he *suddenly felt grateful for them.*"[2]

Just as important as what changed for the Mariner is what did not change. The Mariner did not find a philosophical proof for his new way of seeing. There was no empirical investigation and no hypothesis testing. There was simply an inner change in perspective. Jones writes, "How the world is—the facts of the world—remain as they were. Objects seen 'as it were,' from the midst of them are unaltered. And the task of finding out about them—the task of science—is unaltered."[3] There is no science-religion question here. Whatever science says or does has no bearing on the Mariner's new way of seeing. He feels a part of everything rather than alienated and alone. As Jones says, he feels an "acceptance of life."[4]

I contend that the Mariner's conversion is instructive when it comes to seeing how a religious way of seeing the world functions. On this construal, religion is seen as a way of viewing what is already "out there" by enacting a change on how we interpret the facts of existence. Here is how Wittgenstein puts matters, "It strikes me that a religious belief could only be something like a passionate commitment to a system of reference. Hence, although it's a *belief*, it's really a way of living, or a way of assessing life. It's passionately seizing hold of *this* interpretation."[5] Wittgenstein,

1. Jones, "Love as Perception of Meaning," 151.
2. Ibid. Emphasis in the original.
3. Ibid., 152.
4. Ibid.
5 Wittgenstein, *Culture and Value*, 64. Emphasis in original.

like Jones, takes religion to be, at least in part, a way of seeing the world. Again, this seeing would have very little to do with how science describes things; in fact, this seeing would be a type of religious reflection on the facts of science *however they are described*. I call this way of interpreting religious belief *the religious stance*.

The religious stance can be defined as an attitude taken towards the facts of existence whereby the believer interprets the fact of science as being imbued with grace and love. In a sense this is a way of seeing the world *sub specie aeternitatis*. The religious believer sees the whole of existence as interrelated, not because science has proven this to be so, but because the world, with all its foibles, is still God's world. The direction of seeing is reversed. We do not passively *see* what is there; rather we *interpret* what is there, seeing it from (to borrow a phrase from Wittgenstein) "a religious point of view."[6] This type of seeing is active not passive. Taking religion as a stance stresses the differences between science and religion. In his book *God, a Guide for the Perplexed*, Keith Ward writes, "Scientific explanations help us to predict and control and repeat events under controlled conditions. Talking about God does none of these things, since the purposes of God remain almost wholly unknown to us. It might actually make a difference if there is a God who has some purpose, but we cannot use that theory to help us to predict what is going to happen next. As a scientific hypothesis, God is pretty useless."[7] This does not mean we need to work harder to bolster the hypothesis of God, but rather realize that we are misunderstanding the way the concept of God functions. Before looking at specific examples of questions, which while outside the scope of science are well within the domain of a religious stance, I will explain a bit more clearly just what is (and what is not) entailed by the religious stance.

THE RELIGIOUS STANCE

In his book *On The Meaning Of Life*, John Cottingham hints at what a religious stance may look like when he writes, "Such a [religiously motivated] mindset is hard to describe in purely cognitive terms; for it is not primarily characterisable in terms of propositions assented to, but is a matter of a certain orientation in which emotions and beliefs and practices of worship and moral convictions merge together in what Wittgenstein called

---

6. See, Malcolm, *Wittgenstein: A Religious Point of View? 1.*

7. Ward, *God, a Guide for the Perplexed*, 185.

'a passionate commitment' to a certain form of life."[8] In his 1999 Terry Lectures published as *The Empirical Stance*, Bas van Fraassen makes a similar claim when he writes that "[A]n encounter with God does not involve solving a theoretical equation or answering a factual query; its searing question is an existential demand we face in fear and trembling. As with a human person, the encounter coincides with a call to decision: possible stances toward ourselves and to our world come to the fore and ask for a choice. The choice is momentous and sometimes, in some ways, inescapable, for it pertains to our ultimate concern.[9]

Both Cottingham and van Fraassen offer interesting and relevant possibilities about how we may begin to understand what taking a religious stance towards existence means. I will define the religious stance as having the following three components. First, a religious stance is an existential approach that is taken in the face of various aspects of life. To call such an approach existential is simply to say that it is a voluntary choice, involving both the emotions (passions) and the intellect, to view certain question about human existence from a religious standpoint. This existential attitude entails the tendency to see certain aspects of human existence (such as suffering, death, advancement, and accomplishments) under the purview of religious categories (such as grace, mercy, redemption, and divine love). We may call this the *existential condition* of the religious stance. Second, a religious stance involves an expressive component that reveals itself in the actions and choices of the religious believer. This is simply to say that there is more to religion than simply assenting to the truth of a set of propositions; rather it involves an expression of faith seen in certain characteristic religious practices whether these are solitary or communal. The expressive component of the religious stance is partly a physical manifestation of the existential attitude. We may call this the *expressive condition* of the religious stance. Finally, although the religious stance may get expressed in the form of beliefs (often expressed in propositional form), the religious stance should not be seen as simply the totality of a set of propositions that the believer takes to be true. That being said, any account of religious belief and practice must account for the propositional component of religious language since these propositions *appear* to play such a large role in what we generally think of as a religious

---

8. Cottingham, *On the Meaning of Life*, 74.
9. Van Fraassen, *The Empirical Stance*, 193.

commitment. This is especially important with the religious stance since it claims that religious belief is mainly characterized by "forms of life" in which propositions (taken as statements that are either "true" or "false") play only a minor role. With a broader account of religious propositions forthcoming, we can at least say that the religious stance has an important propositional component that I will call the *propositional condition* of the religious stance. As a way of developing the idea of a religious stance in a more philosophically interesting way, I will look at each of these conditions in turn.

EXPRESSING A RELIGIOUS COMMITMENT

While many philosophers want to separate the expressive component of religious belief from its propositional component (for reasons that we will look at shortly), the religious stance takes them as two different, but related, ways of doing the same thing (namely, taking a religious stance towards existence). How this is so will take a bit of explaining.

The Practical Side of the Religious Stance

There are many possible ways that religious individuals express their faith, and while it is impossible to list all of them here it seems appropriate (and warranted) to list a few common traits that many "garden-variety" religious individuals possess to some degree or another. While what follows is certainly not exhaustive, it may be seen as a fairly general set of characteristically religious attitudes and practices.[10]

First, many garden-variety religious individuals see life as a gift bequeathed to them from a divine presence. This attitude allows believers to see the world, despite its obvious vicissitudes, as a place "transfigured by that beauty and goodness and truth."[11] Such an attitude is often exhibited by seeing the world as a place where all that happens falls within the purview of the divine to whom the proper response is an attitude of thankfulness, praise or worship. This attitude is often expressed in the belief that life as a whole is penetrated (or "shot-through") with moments of grace in

---

10. Noting the following marks of religiosity are not unique to me, but are rather an amalgam of some of the views expressed by Robert Coburn and John Cottingham. See, Coburn, *The Strangeness of the Ordinary*, 128–30 and, Cottingham, *On the Meaning of Life*, 90–91.

11. Cottingham, *On the Meaning of Life,* 90.

which individual choices are sometimes taken as manifestations of divine guidance (or at least divine approval). Seeing the world as a gift, while not shying away from its more troubling aspects, often gives rise to the idea that there are no "irredeemably tragic situations, no situations of horror from which there is 'no exit' . . ."[12] These attitudes do not always (or even often) lead the believer to give an explanation or philosophical justification for how God will ultimately redeem the injustice in the world (although this may occur); rather, it often manifests in the attitude that nothing (not even death) can be of ultimate harm to the righteous. This attitude may also manifest in the (possibly fleeting) feeling that Wittgenstein described in his "Lecture on Ethics" as "the state of mind in which one is inclined to say 'I am safe, nothing can injure me whatever happens.'"[13]

Second, to express a religious attitude is, at least for many, to take human responsibility as a vital and important fact of being human. This responsibility may show up in a variety of ways; however, a typically religious attitude towards moral responsibility tends to manifest in characteristic attitudes towards the poor and needy. This means individuals will often attempt to alleviate unnecessary suffering whether this happens through charity work, giving to worthy causes or choosing careers that are oriented towards service to others. Robert Coburn writes, "In short, their [believers] behavior exhibits the kind of orientation depicted by the picture of Christ in the Gospels, the orientation of the self-sacrificing healer of the physical and spiritual ailments of others."[14] This attitude of responsibility for the poor and needy often manifests itself conversely in an attitude of frugality towards "worldly excesses" and restraint towards the desire to seek worldly fame. Along with having such an attitude towards those in need, a typical (though not universal) attitude is to see the striving after worldly riches as somehow shallow and sub-par. Cottingham refers to this attitude using the New Testament term *metanoia*, which he describes as "a fundamental shift in outlook, liberating us from anxious care about wealth and position, and leading us to a kind of 'rebirth' in which life will be lived 'more abundantly,' as freely as the 'birds of the air' or the 'lilies of the field,' unclogged by concern with outward show and

---

12. Coburn, *The Strangeness of the Ordinary*, 129.

13. Wittgenstein, *Philosophical Occasions*, 41.

14. Coburn, *The Strangeness of the Ordinary*, 34.

image."[15] This attitude is essentially a way of turning away from our own selfish ego and turning towards others in an expression of agapeistic love.

Third, many religious believers are gripped by a feeling that existence is somehow sacred, something that transcends the mundane. This mystical-type experience has been described in various ways throughout the history of religion. In Christian theology, the German theologian Friedrich Schleiermacher, known for his description of theology as being primarily a matter of "feeling," stated that at the root of all theological inquiry lies the feeling of "absolute dependence." In *The Christian Faith*, he writes, "The feeling of absolute dependence, accordingly, is not to be explained as an awareness of the world's existence, but only as an awareness of the existence of God, as the absolute undivided unity."[16] The theologian Rudolf Otto believed that a non-rational encounter with what he called the "numinous" produced a type of experience he described as *mysterium tremendum et fascinosum*.[17] This experience is often characterized by a certain fearfulness (awe or dread) as well as by feeling that one is in contact with a great mystery. Again, these expressions of an encounter with the divine do not differ greatly from Wittgenstein relating certain moments in his life when he felt "absolutely safe." In whatever way these experiences get expressed, they play a major role in the life of many religious believers.

Finally, many religious individuals express their faith in some ritual or cultic practices often described as "worship," "prayer," "meditation," or "celebration." Such practices may involve public worship, the singing of hymns, or meeting at set times to gather for communal prayer or meditation. They may also involve the celebration of certain holy days with others who are part of the same faith community or the ritual celebration of milestone moments in life such as birth, marriage and death. Oftentimes the ritual expressions of religious faith can take the form of communal works of charity where the "faithful" pool their resources to help those in need. While many of these ritualistic and cultic practices of faith can be public, there are also private expressions of faith. Individuals may pray before eating a meal, set time aside each day for meditating on sacred texts, or participate in individual works of charity whereby faith is ex-

---

15. Cottingham, *On the Meaning of Life*, 101–2.

16. Schleiermacher, *The Christian Faith*, 132.

17. See Otto, *The Idea of the Holy*, chapter 4.

pressed in giving time (or money) to those in need. Whatever the extent of such ritual practices, it is fairly clear that such practices make up an important part of the expression of religious faith, so much so that it would be hard to imagine an individual assenting to belief without engaging in these practices to some extent or another.

In some ways many may take these various forms of religious expression as obvious, the problem is that many of the same individuals also think that such practices are senseless if they are not grounded in true propositions about the nature of reality. I want to suggest, however, that there is a way to interpret the propositional content of religious beliefs (such as "God exists," "Jesus rose from the dead," or "In the beginning God created the heavens") as also being expressions of attitudes and not simply claims about what exists.

The Propositional Side of Religion

Some individuals claim that attitudes and practices expressed by religious believers make sense only if the believer first assents to the truth of the doctrinal propositions; otherwise, they insist, why would believers bother living a religious life? Does not the choice to live a religious life first depend on fixing the truth-value of the religious doctrines? But do we need to see religious believers as being committed to believing a set of straightforward factual propositions when they assent to the truth of doctrinal statements such as "Jesus rose from the dead," "God created the heavens and the earth," or even "God exists"? An account of religious belief that can avoid conflict with the natural sciences requires an account of religious doctrines that can interpret believing in them as accomplishing something *other than* believing that a certain set of facts obtain.

In his introductory text on philosophy of religion, B. R. Tilghman writes,

> Much misunderstanding of religion is the result of supposing that to be religious is largely a matter of believing that certain *propositions* are true, propositions whose only difference from other kinds of propositions is that they are about supernatural rather than natural facts. This misunderstanding is exhibited from both outside and inside religion. It leads the religious outsider, the non-believer, to dismiss religion and religious people as foolish. It has led some religious people to try to support their beliefs with arguments and evidence, but, since the arguments are invariably

bad and the "evidence" cannot stand up to scholarly and scientific standards, they end up making themselves foolish.[18]

It seems that Tilghman is essentially correct here. If religion is primarily a matter of defending religious propositions by presenting evidence that can be evaluated in terms similar to the way that empirical facts are investigated, then religious belief tends to look paltry compared to its scientific counterparts. However, if an account of religious doctrines can be given that avoids seeing them as pseudo-scientific, then judging them by the standards of the sciences would be a mistake. Can such an account of religious propositions be offered? Indeed it can. However, before proceeding to that task, it will be helpful to look at the distinction, made by Tilghman, between "believing that" and "believing in."[19]

Generally speaking, to believe "that" something is the case is simply to believe that it obtains, is a fact, or is true. In this case to believe that "flying dodos exist" is simply to believe it true (or factual) that flying dodos exist. To believe that "Chicago is the largest city in Illinois" is to believe it indeed to be the case that Chicago is the largest city in Illinois. However, when someone states "I believe *in* democracy" or "I believe *in* God," they are not claiming that "democracy" or "God" is merely an existent fact; rather, they are claiming to have a certain level of trust in the efficacy (or goodness) of "democracy" or "God." In this case to believe "*that x*" commits one to a certain ontological stance toward the existence of *x*, while believing "*in x*" commits one to an existential (in the philosophical not the logical sense) stance towards *x*.

It is a misunderstanding of the distinction between believing-in and believing-that that gives rise to the following objection. It would appear obvious, so the objection goes, that in order to believe "*in x,*" an individual must first believe (or have established) "*that* x exists" is true. It would be odd (would it not?) to say, "I believe in Barack Obama" but "I do not believe that it is true that Barack Obama exists"? To believe "in Obama" commits one to (or is parasitic on) the belief that it is true that Obama actually exists. Or, to put the matter in religious terms, John Searle writes, "The reason people play the language game of religion is because they think there is something outside the language game that

---

18. Tilghman, *An Introduction to the Philosophy of Religion*, 209.

19. Ibid., 208–18.

gives it a point."[20] So doesn't believing in God commit one to the prior belief in the truth of the proposition that "God exists"? Tilghman answers, "Paradoxical as it may seem, in order to believe in God we do not first have to establish that God exists. There may not be anything at all that can be called 'establishing that God exists.'"[21] This is because no empirical fact could establish such a claim, nor, at least for the believer, could any empirical fact falsify it. If the reality of God is not an empirical fact, it makes little sense to talk about establishing the fact of God's existence as if it were another "fact" on par with those found in the sciences. Of course, believing in God is not a fact in the scientific sense at all (since it is supposed to represent a "spiritual truth"); it is, however, a fact that shows itself in the life of the believer. In a sense, when it comes to the existence of God, ontology and epistemology conflate in such a way that to see what is meant by the claim that God exists is to see what is meant when a believer claims to live a certain way and hold certain attitudes towards the conditions of life. Or, what amounts to the same thing, when it comes to the special case of "believing in God," the object that one refers to conflates with the practice that surrounds the claim to believe. In this case we may say, with Paul Tillich, that God does not exist, except in the sense that there are religious people and religious attitudes (or, if you will, a religious conceptual scheme).[22] D. Z. Phillips writes, "In learning by contemplation, attention, renunciation, what forgiving, thanking, loving, etc., mean in these [religious] contexts, the believer is participating in the reality of God; *this is what we mean by God's reality.*"[23] This may bring up the objection that religious belief amounts to *nothing more* than the claim that "People exist that have religious attitudes." This is the exact claim that was constantly leveled against D. Z. Phillips and his Wittgensteinian approach to religion. John Hick puts the objections this way, "I take him [Phillips] to imply that this concept of God does not answer to any reality beyond human language and human forms of life. One can further clarify this reading of Phillips by noting its implication that before there were any humans there was no God, for God exists only as a factor in our

20. Magee, *The Great Philosophers: An Introduction to Western Philosophy* (BBC, 1987), 345. Quoted in Phillips, *Wittgenstein and Religion*, 23.

21. Tilghman, *An Introduction to the Philosophy of Religion*, 210.

22. See Tillich, *Systematic Theology*, vol. 1.

23. Phillips, *Death and Immortality*, 55. Emphasis in original.

religious language and behaviour."[24] Phillips replies, "In order to say that God is our creator, who existed before the mountains were brought forth, or the earth was made, we would have to participate in the religious form in which this confession has its sense. But in making the confession, we would not be saying anything about language. We would not be saying that a 'factor in our language' existed before the mountains were brought forth. We would be confessing God as our creator."[25] But what does it mean to confess God as creator? Phillips continues, "Where are we to look to see what these beliefs amount to? Where else but in the direction that Hick resists, to the language and form of life in which the belief has its sense. This is not to deny God's independent existence. It is precisely to see what talk of 'independent existence' comes to in these religious beliefs."[26] The appearance that one is denying the *real* existence of God when one looks to the meaning of the use of religious concepts may be an unfortunate by-product of thinking that religious concepts *must* function like their empirical counterparts. Yet, if religious utterances are not, in any straightforward sense, "fact-stating," then what sense can we make of religious propositions?

I suggest that we take the propositional doctrines of faith as serving as linguistic expressions that express, in propositional form, feelings and attitudes directed toward a spiritual reality. In this case, propositional expressions of faith will be no different than the expressions found in rituals and other cultic practices, it is just that these expressions take the shape of propositions that can be mistaken for factual claims. If doctrines play this role, then they will not be vastly different from the other ways of expressing faith mentioned above. Coburn writes, "[s]ome people who live the life of faith view the religious language that pervades their worship services as analogous to the music such services involve and to the ritualistic bodily movement that often accompany the verbal acts they engage in, and hence as no more expressive of propositional content—of thoughts that are capable of truth and falsity in a straightforward sense— than this music and these bodily movements are.[27] While doctrines may show up in propositional form, they function more as regulative pictures

24. Hick, "Critique of D. Z. Phillips," in Stephan T. Davis, *Encountering Evil*, 162. Quoted in Phillips *The Problem of Evil*, 170.

25. Ibid., 171.

26. Ibid.

27. Coburn, *The Strangeness of the Ordinary*, 133.

that religious believers hold before their minds to remind them of certain aspects of their religious stance; they express in propositional form the believers existential religious commitment. They are verbal expressions tantamount to a confession of faith. When a believer states that "God exists" or "God created the world" they are taking a certain attitude towards existence as a whole, not making an empirical statement on par with "a tenth planet exists" or "Joe created a new chemical in the lab." To not understand these differences is to exhibit the same sort of spiritual tone-deafness exhibited by those that practice religious scientism.

All of this should not be taken to mean that the believer has nothing to say about the natural world. Indeed as long as the believer takes this world to be the creation of God, they will always take a religious stance towards the facts that science investigates and explains. However, this does not mean that science and religion are in competition, or even that they are doing anything close to the same thing. In closing, I want to look at a few characteristic ways that the religious stance appears at the fringes (or limits) of scientific investigation.

RELIGION AND LIFE'S CONDITIONS

When it comes to the relationship between science and religion, there are two places we can look. First, we may want to stress the way that religious believers interpret the work that science does. For example, believers may look on the work of the scientist as evidence of divine design or examples that God acts. However, as I have tried to show in the preceding chapters, these interpretations should not be taken as having the same linguistic (or logical) function as the work the scientist does. Thinking that there is some sort of logical overlap is what often leads to the types of conceptual confusions exhibited by religious scientism. Second, there are ways that religious believers talk about certain aspects of the created world that do not, even *in principle*, overlap with the work of the sciences. This isn't only because religious believers are using language in a different way than the scientist, but also because they are attempting to provide answers to questions that only arise at the limits of science. In fact, even using the term "question" may be problematic since it opens the door for confusing a religious answer with an empirical one. The questions I have in mind are actually more like what have been called "limiting questions." They are questions that appear to be asking for an empirical answer but in actuality are better seen as statements about existence that require an existential stance. D. Z. Phillips writes that these "are questions born out of bewilderment at the contingencies of life."[28] In what follows I want to look at three different examples of such limiting questions, paying close attention to how these are the types of questions that are open to a religious stance while remaining essentially outside the explanatory reach of science.

Something Rather Than Nothing

In the *Tractatus* Wittgenstein writes, "It is not how things are in the world that is mystical, but that it [the world] exists."[29] Wittgenstein was not expressing a perplexity about any specific state of affairs *within* the world, but rather a certain wonder that anything at all should exist. This question is generally posed as "Why is there something rather than nothing?" While this may appear to be a request for a factual answer (like "Why are there seven ducks on the pond today?" or "Why was the flight so late?"), it is often posed not as a request for information, but as an exclamation of awe, wonder, or perplexity in the face of existence itself. In this sense the question is better seen as an instance of what D. Z. Phillips above called a "limiting question"; or a form of question that is not asking for an explanation as much as it is a statement that is "born of bewilderment at the contingencies of life."[30] There are two reasons why it seems best to interpret the question "Why is there something rather than nothing?" as a type of limiting question.

First, to think that the question is a request for the type of answer that science is capable of providing is to misunderstand the nature of the question. For example, if someone were to state that the question "Why is there something rather than nothing?" is exactly the type of question that scientific cosmology is attempting to answer, it would seem that they have misunderstood (or are miss-applying) the concept of "nothing." Peter van Inwagen addresses such a misunderstanding when he writes, "Surrounding the word 'nothing' with double quotes makes the word look as if it were supposed to function as a sort of nickname for a vast emptiness or an enormous vacuum. But to regard the word 'nothing' as

---

28. Phillips, *The Problem of God*, 131.

29. Wittgenstein, *Tractatus Logico-Philosophicus*, 6.44.

30. Phillips, *The Problem of Evil*, 131.

functioning in that way would be to misunderstand it. To say that there is nothing is to say that there isn't *anything*, not even a vast emptiness."[31]

Despite the meaning of "nothing" utilized by both philosophy and common sense, some may still want to dig in their heels and insist that scientific cosmology is capable of offering a solution to the problem (after all aren't they interested in the question of "origins"?). This often takes the form of an appeal to quantum fluctuations occurring in a vacuum (as suggested by Edward Tryon and Alexander Vilenkin) or an appeal to the revised version of Stephen Hawking's "no-boundary condition"[32] offered by Hawking and James Hartle. Recently, Hawking, desiring to match some of his fellow scientists as playing the role of bad theologian, writes, "Because there is a law like . . . gravity, the universe can and will create itself from nothing . . . Spontaneous creation is the reason there is something rather than nothing, why the universe exists, why we exist." Further, "It is not necessary to invoke God to light the blue touch paper and set the universe going."[33] But are these cosmological explanations actually an instance of something coming from nothing? It would again appear that this depends on what we take "nothing" to mean. If nothing is allowed to contain something, then maybe cosmology is answering some question about the move from "nothing" to "something," but it is not the same question that is under discussion here. The odd use of the term "nothing" by contemporary cosmology is what John Polkinghorne is chiding when he writes, "The quantum vacuum is a hive of activity, full of fluctuations, random comings-to-be and fading away. . . . Suppose for a moment that such a fluctuation was the actual origin of our universe. It would certainly not have come from something which without great abuse of language could be called 'nothing.'"[34] It isn't that cosmology is not interested in origins (they surely are), it is just that in talking about *nothing*, they appear to be using a different concept than the one most philosophers (and theologians) are interested in. A nothing that contains something may be of interest in physics, but it amounts to nonsense in philosophy.

31. Peter van Inwagen, *Metaphysics*, 72. Emphasis in original.

32. Stephen Hawking, *A Brief History of Time*.

33. Hawking, *The Grand Design*, 180.

34. Polkinghorne, *One World*. Quoted in Worthing, *God, Creation and Contemporary Physics*, 73.

Second, all of this semantic finger pointing, while justified, may be unnecessary. It may be that when an individual is asking the question "Why is there something rather than nothing?" they are asking a question that not only may not be able to be answered by science, but one that can (and will) still be asked even if science could provide an answer. In this case, whatever answer is given would not satisfy the inquirer since the question can still be meaningfully posed no matter what answer science delivers. This isn't simply because the questioner is being stubborn, but because the nature of the question being asked is such that it is possible (as I noted above) that what is being asked is not simply a straightforward empirical question but a perplexity that can be posed no matter what answer is given. If the scientist (or metaphysician) states that the world is such that it must be x, one may still feel compelled to ask why the world is that way. In this case the question may be translated (as Terry Eagleton suggests) as "How come the cosmos?"[35] While this may not be the type of question that science can (even in principle) answer, it is a question that allows for a religious response, as John Cottingham writes, "We may have reached the limits of science here, but perhaps we have not necessarily reached the limits of human discourse. There is a rich tradition of religious language, both in our western culture and elsewhere that grapples with the task of addressing what cannot be fully captured by even the most complete scientific account of the phenomenal world."[36]

Death and Human Finitude

Another perplexity (at least for some) regarding the nature of human life that often provokes a religious response is the fact of human finitude; or the fact that human life ends in death. This may be taken globally as the claim that all human life (as we know it) will one day be extinct (maybe when the sun engulfs the earth), or it can be taken as the more personal claim that my life (and the life of those I love) will someday end in death. It is the personal view of our own death (or the death of our loved ones) that seems more apt to cause existential strife; more so, that is, than the global claim that some day in the far-off future, civilization will become extinct. This is because our own death is more imminent and personal than the long-term extinction of the race as a whole. Pascal pointedly

---

35. Eagleton, *The Meaning of Life*, 3.
36. Cottingham, *On the Meaning of Life*, 8.

describes the human condition *vis-à-vis* the realization of our death when he writes, "Let us imagine a number of men in chains, and all condemned to death, where some are killed each day in the sight of the others, and those who remain see their own fate in that of their fellows, and wait their turn, looking at each other sorrowfully and without hope."[37] According to Pascal, the problem of our finitude is exacerbated as we see others precede us in death and realize that we ourselves are rushing (or crawling) towards the same fate. The realization of the personal claim of death caused profound shock to the psyche of Ivan Ilyich in Tolstoy's famous novel *The Death of Ivan Ilyich*. After realizing in a shocking way that it was *he* himself who was dying, Tolstoy puts the following powerful and touching thoughts in the head of Ivan:

> Ivan Ilych saw that he was dying, and he was in continual despair. In the depth of his heart he knew he was dying, but not only was he not accustomed to the thought, he simply did not and could not grasp it. The syllogism he had learnt from Kiesewetter's Logic: "Caius is a man, men are mortal, therefore Caius is mortal," had always seemed to him correct as applied to Caius, but certainly not as applied to himself. That Caius—man in the abstract—was mortal, was perfectly correct, but he was not Caius, not an abstract man, but a creature quite, quite separate from all others. He had been little Vanya, with a mamma and a papa, with Mitya and Volodya, with the toys, a coachman and a nurse, afterwards with Katenka and will all the joys, griefs, and delights of childhood, boyhood, and youth. What did Caius know of the smell of that striped leather ball Vanya had been so fond of? Had Caius kissed his mother's hand like that, and did the silk of her dress rustle so for Caius? Had he rioted like that at school when the pastry was bad? Had Caius been in love like that? Could Caius preside at a session as he did? Caius really was mortal, and it was right for him to die; but for me, little Vanya, Ivan Ilych, with all my thoughts and emotions, it's altogether a different matter. It cannot be that I ought to die. That would be too terrible.[38]

Death in the abstract was not a problem for Ivan, in fact he knew the logical syllogism well enough to know that indeed "all men are mortal." What he failed to realize (as many people do) is that *he* was included in

37. Pascal, *Pensees,*§ 199. Quoted in Placher, *Readings in the History of Christian Theology*, 54–55.

38. Tolystoy, *The Death of Ivan Ilyich*, 137.

the set of "all." This realization created a state of terror and despair. The range of feelings this realization lends itself to has been the topic of many philosophical works. Kierkegaard avers: "Speed on you, you drama of life, which no one calls a comedy, no one a tragedy, because no one ever saw the end! Speed on, you drama of existence, where life cannot be spent again any more than money! Why did no one ever return from the dead? Because life does not know how to trap one as death does, because life has no persuasive power like those of death."[39] Paul Tillich, not known for his clear writing style, clearly states, "the anxiety of death overshadows all concrete anxieties and gives them their ultimate seriousness."[40] Finally, John Cottingham writes, "The very ability to see the implications of our finite nature so acutely, means that, alone among the rest of creation, we cannot wholly be at rest, we cannot be entirely at home in the world."[41]

As noted, the fact that humans come to some acute realization of their own mortality does not mean that a religious response must be sought. Responses may vary from a yawn to anger to the use of Botox or exercise to stave off the reminders of our physical decay. However, a religious response would seem natural, especially if it was formed as a response to the possibility that death may mark the extinction of our consciousness. Of course, the form such a religious response takes may range from the banal to the poetic. Some responses argue for the metaphysical possibility of post-mortem survival as if mere survival were somehow automatically a religious response (haven't they seen the *Twilight* movies?). Of course, philosophical arguments for survival of death may simply be an intellectual way to placate our fears by convincing ourselves that "life goes on" (even if it continues in a place very far away and with a very different body, or no body at all). D. Z. Phillips has called such discussions of eternal life "temporal immortality" because they tend to do little more than extend our current finite existence indefinitely into the future.[42] However, as Phillips notes, religion is not limited to this response. In a wonderful passage from *Recovering Religious Concepts*, he writes, "At death, it is tempting to see it as an easy way out; to turn one's back on one's life with all its imperfections. But that is not what Christianity asks of us. It offers

39. Kierkegaard, *Fear and Trembling*, 176. Quoted in George Pattison, *The Philosophy of Kierkegaard*, 68.

40. Tillich, *The Courage to Be*, 43.

41. Cottingham, *On the Meaning of Life*, 78.

42. See Phillips, *Recovering Religious Concepts*, chapter 9.

a hope that the believer, with all his weakness, becomes more than he or she could ever be by their own efforts. This is what happens at death if it is offered to God. . . . The death of the believer is placed in God's hands. Notice the nature of the promise; that where God is, there will we be also, God is a spiritual reality. We become more than ourselves at death when we become part of that spiritual reality."[43] On Phillips's reading, the goal of death goes beyond the mere survival of our consciousness, to stressing the idea that death takes on a religious significance as believers offer their lives back to God. On this view death is not simply equated with an afterlife, but taken as the ultimate (or penultimate) act of consecrating one's life to God. Whether or not this attitude actually develops in all (or even the majority of) believers, does not hamper the fact that our finitude is an impetus for developing (and nurturing) a religious stance towards our own finite existence.

As with the question about why there is something rather than nothing, some may want to say that far from having nothing to say about death and human finitude, science appears to have much to say. Science, especially medicine, can tell us about how the dying process occurs, what the process will feel like in certain instances, or even why individuals tend to have certain types of "near death experiences." Some of these very topics are the exact types of things addressed in Sherwin Nuland's book *How We Die*.[44] Furthermore, evolutionary biologists can explain (to some extent) why death is a natural part of the process of evolution, possibly even explaining the benefits that individual deaths have to the species as a whole.[45] Given the fact that science touches on the question of death in this way, it is surely an odd claim (so the argument goes) to say that human finitude is a question not addressed by the sciences.

This type of argument, however, misses the point. To see why, take the following example offered by Rush Rhees. Rhees writes, "Suppose there has been an earthquake, and geologists now give an explanation of it. This will not be an answer to the woman who has lost her home and her child and asks 'Why?' It does not make it easier to understand 'what has befallen us.' And the woman's question, though it may drive her mad, does not seek an answer."[46] In this story, it isn't that the mother simply

---

43. Ibid., 154.
44. Nuland, *How We Die*.
45. See, for example, Stanley Shostak, *The Evolution of Death*.
46. Rhees, *Without Answers*, 16–17.

shuts her mind off to the *correct* answer regarding what has happened to her child; rather, the answer does not even begin to address the issue she is grappling with. She knows *how* her child died, she now wants to know *why*. I believe something similar is in place when we think about science and human finitude. More information about what will happen to us physiologically as we die, or even more information about why death is a necessary part of evolution, does not address the issue of how I am to face the fact of my own death. The anxiety is caused by the fact that I am facing the possibility of non-existence; I am facing the possible extinction of all that I know and love. My conscious experience may simply fizzle out like a candle flame extinguished between a moistened thumb and forefinger. This is the type of problem that philosophers like Pascal, Kierkegaard, and Tillich (and many more) are wrestling with. Certainly more information about the biology of death will not alleviate the type of anxiety that comes with recognition of our own personal finitude (in fact it may make such anxiety worse.). The clash is between my awareness of my own existence and the possibility that death may represent its annihilation; it is this realization that serves as a possible impetus for the development of a religious stance. John Cottingham summarizes this point well when he writes, "If the origin of the spiritual impulse is the gap between what we are and what we aspire to be, then since, as long as we remain finite, neither science nor anything else can close that gap, the only available resource will be some kind of interior modification which will enable us to come to terms with it."[47]

The Meaning of It All

One final aspect of human existence serves as fertile ground for the development of a religious stance—the fact that asking about the meaning of life as-a-whole remains a viable (and open) question. This is among the questions that remain unanswerable by the natural sciences, not because of some defect on the part of science, but because it slips outside the domain of the questions that science is prepared to answer. As John Cottingham writes, "The situation . . . is that the scientist offers an account of how things happened . . . and it then remains a separate (and so far open) question whether the events and processes so established can

47. Cottinghman, *On the Meaning of Life*, 79.

reasonably be interpreted as manifesting the power and purposes of a divine creator."[48]

At the end of his book, *The First Three Minutes*, Physicist Steven Weinberg writes, "It is almost irresistible for humans to believe that we have some special relation to the universe, that human life is not just a more-or-less farcical outcome of a chain of accidents reaching back to the first three minutes, but that we were somehow built from the beginning . . . It is hard to realize that this all [i.e., life on Earth] is just a tiny part of an overwhelmingly hostile universe. It is even harder to realize that this present universe has evolved from an unspeakably unfamiliar early condition, and faces a future extinction of endless cold or intolerable heat. The more the universe seems comprehensible, the more it also seems pointless."[49] Weinberg's sentiments are not part and parcel of anything he learned as a physicist, but rather representative of something standing much closer to metaphysics (or scientism) than physics. However, his feelings are natural given the success of the sciences and the tendency to want to extend the scope of science to reality as a whole. If human consciousness is simply part of the natural (albeit random) chance processes that happened to result from the combination of matter plus a whole lot of time, then it is hard to think Weinberg's views are unjustified. As God slowly gets pushed out of the center of the explanatory gap, it is normal to feel that ultimate meaning may have the same fate.

Weinberg's "pointless" universe is not only a viable option, but it is one that is certainly not restricted to individuals operating from the standpoint of the success of science. In Macbeth, Shakespeare writes,

> Life's but a fleeting shadow, a poor player
> That struts and frets his hour upon the stage
> And then is heard no more. It is a tale
> Told by an idiot, full of sound and fury,
> Signifying . . . nothing.[50]

Even Leo Tolstoy was not immune to the feeling that all of life may simply be for naught. In his famous *Confessions*, Tolstoy relates how he reached a point in his life after achieving a certain level of success when he began to question whether his life had any real meaning. He writes, "In my search

---

48. Ibid., 46.

49. Weinberg, *The First Three Minutes*, 149.

50. Shakespeare, *Macbeth* Act 5, Scene 5. Quoted in Cottingham, *On the Meaning of Life*, 103.

after the question of life I experienced the same feeling which a man who has lost his way in the forest may experience. He comes to a clearing, climbs a tree, and clearly sees an unlimited space before him; at the same time he sees that there are no houses there, and that there can be none; he goes back to the forest, into the darkness, and he sees darkness and again there are no houses.[51] There seems to be a bit of parity between Tolstoy's statement here and Weinberg's quote above. However, Tolstoy seems to take a vastly different approach to dealing with the question of life's meaninglessness. After wrestling with whether a religious response to the problem of meaninglessness is a viable option, Tolstoy writes, "No matter what answers faith may give, its every answer gives to the finite existence of man the sense of the infinite,—a sense which is not destroyed by suffering, privation and death."[52] Weinberg and Tolstoy seem to feel the pull of the same question, although they arrive at very different ways to deal with it. It is not that one is following science "whither so ever it leads" and the other has leapt into the irrational world of faith. It is rather that when faced with a question not answerable by science, they chose different stances. Whatever brings individuals to deal with the question of life's meaning, the religious response remains a viable option.

As already mentioned several times, circumstances and questions (i.e., Why does anything exist? How should I confront my own finitude? Is life meaningful?), do not automatically call for a religious response. Many atheists have proffered responses to such questions with intellectual honesty and academic tenacity. Yet, even if a religious stance is not required, it continues to be a live option (in a Jamesian sense), since the questions (and facts of existence) that are being dealt with are open to many philosophical and metaphysical interpretations (including a religious one). The viability of the religious stance is also bolstered by the fact that such questions remain (and barring a reformation in our meaning of "science" *must* remain) outside of the explanatory scope of the sciences.

PRACTICING SCIENCE AND PRACTICING RELIGION

What has been said here about the religious stance will be uninteresting to the defender of scientism (both religious and secular), since they either relegate knowledge to what science reveals or see religion as be-

---

51. Tolstoy, *My Confession,* in Klemke, *The Meaning of Life,* 13.

52. Ibid., 17.

ing in the same logical category as science such that science can aid religion in its quest for legitimacy. However, this is to ignore the types of questions that a religious stance is attempting to deal with. Existence, death, and finitude are not comfortable dinnertime discussion topics, but neither are they so trivial that they can (or should) be avoided. If one discipline is not equipped to deal with such topics, then it seems odd to criticize those who recognize this fact and look elsewhere for an answer. The defender of scientism (not the scientist) appears to be like the child who became angry because everyone won't stay and play in their sandbox, however, it may be that the sandbox is not conducive to the game that is being played. In this case there is some justification in looking for a different place to play.

Earlier, I quoted John Cottingham as saying, "if the origin of the supernatural impulse is the gap between what we are and what we aspire to be, then since, as long as we remain finite, neither science or anything else can close the gap, the only available resource will be some kind of radical interior modification which will enable us to come to terms with it."[53] Later in the same work he continues, "The plea is for an acknowledgement that human beings, in their vulnerability and finitude, need, in order to survive, modes of responding to the world which go beyond what is disclosed in a rational scientific analysis of the relevant phenomena."[54] In this case, the argument is not against science. It is not an attempt to get others to see science as just one way of obtaining knowledge when other ways would have done equally well. Science is often successful (by its own standards) at investigating the empirical world that we inhabit, and this, of course, should be acknowledged. My argument in this book has simply been that in not recognizing the limits of science and the function of religious language, individuals who practice the form of *religious scientism* outlined in this work are trying to force both science and religion to play a role they are not meant to play. Furthermore, insisting that science *can* do such a job is to leave science itself behind and enter the world of scientism. This is a practice that stems partly from ignorance, but mostly from a desire to see religion enjoy the academic prestige that science has achieved. This desire to "worship at the altar of science" not only leads to bad theology, but also to a certain disrespect for the science that these individuals say the adore.

53. Cottingham, *On the Meaning of Life*, 79.
54. Ibid., 99.

Bibliography

Armstrong, David. "Naturalism, Materialism, and First Philosophy." *Philosophia* 8 (1978) 261–76.

Arrington, Robert L., and Hans-Johann Glock. *Wittgenstein and Quine*. London: Routledge, 1996.

Balashov, Yuri, and Alexander Rosenberg. *Myths, Models, and Paradigms: A Comparative Study in Science and Religion*. New York: Harper & Row, 1974.

———. *Philosophy of Science: Contemporary Readings*. New York: Routledge, 2002.

———. *Religion and Science: Historical and Contemporary Issues*. San Francisco: Harper San Francisco, 1997.

Bergstrom, Lars. "Quine, Underdetermination, and Skepticism." *Journal of Philosophy* 90.7 (1993) 331–58.

Berlinski, David. *The Devil's Delusion*. New York: Basic, 2009.

Black, Max. *Models and Metaphors: Studies in Language and Philosophy*. Ithaca, NY: Cornell University Press, 1962.

Block, Ned. "Do Causal Powers Drain Away?" *Philosophy and Phenomenological Research* 67 (1) 133–50.

Carroll, Lewis. *Through the Looking Glass*. No page numbers. Public Domain Books. Kindle Edition.

Chalmers, David. "What is a Neural Correlate of Consciousness?" In *Neural Correlates of Consciousness: Empirical and Conceptual Questions*, edited by Thomas Metzinger, 17–41. Cambridge: MIT, 2000.

Clayton, Philip. *Adventures in the Spirit: God, World, Divine Action*. Edited by Zachary R. Simpson. Minneapolis, MN: Fortress, 2008.

———. "Conceptual Foundations of Emergence Theory." In *The Re-Emergence of Emergence: The Emergentist Hypothesis from Science to Religion*, edited by Philip Clayton and Paul Davies, 1–34. Oxford: Oxford University Press, 2006.

———. *Explanation from Physics to Theology: An Essay in Rationality and Religion*. New Haven, CT: Yale University Press, 1989.

———. *God and Contemporary Science*. Edinburgh Studies in Constructive Theology. Grand Rapids: Eerdmans, 1997.

———. *In Quest of Freedom: The Emergence of Spirit in the Natural World*. Göttingen:Vandenhoeck & Ruprecht, 2009.

———. *Mind and Emergence: From Quantum to Consciousness*. Oxford: Oxford University Press, 2004.

———. "Neuroscience, the Person, and God: An Emergentist Account." *Zygon* 35.3 (2000) 613–52.

Clayton, Philip, and A. R. Peacocke. *In Whom We Live and Move and Have Our Being: Panentheistic Reflections on God's Presence in a Scientific World*. Grand Rapids: Eerdmans, 2004.

Coburn, Robert C. *The Strangeness of the Ordinary: Problems and Issues in Contemporary Metaphysics*. Savage, MD: Rowman & Littlefield, 1990.

Connell, Richard J. *From Observables to Unobservables in Science and Philosophy*. New York: University Press of America, 2000.

Cooper, John. *Panentheism: The Other God of the Philosophers—From Plato to the Present*. Grand Rapids: Baker Academic, 2006.

Corner, David. "Miracles." No pages. § 11. Online: http://www.iep.utm.edu/miracles/.

Cottingham, John. *On the Meaning of Life*. Thinking in Action. New York: Routledge, 2003.

Davies, Paul, and Niels Henrik Gregerson. *Information and the Nature of Reality: From Physics to Metaphysics*. Cambridge: Cambridge University Press, 2010.

Dawkins, Richard. *The Blind Watchmaker: Why the Evidence of Evolution Reveals a Universe Without Design*. New York: Norton, 1987.

————. *A Devil's Chaplain: Reflections on Hope, Lies, Science, and Love*. Boston: Mifflin, 2003.

Dembski, William A. *The Design Revolution: Answering the Toughest Questions About Intelligent Design*. Downers Grove, IL: InterVarsity, 2004.

————. *Intelligent Design: The Bridge between Science & Theology*. Downers Grove, IL: InterVarsity, 1999.

————. *No Free Lunch: Why Specified Complexity Cannot Be Purchased Without Intelligence*. Lanham, MD: Rowman & Littlefield, 2002.

Eagleton, Terry. *The Meaning of Life*. Oxford: Oxford University Press, 2007.

Elsberry, John S. Wilkins, and R. Wesley. "The Advantages of Theft over Toil: The Design Inference and Arguing from Ignorance." *Biology and Philosophy* 16 (2001) 711–24.

Faust, Jennifer. "Can Religious Arguments Persuade?" *International Journal for Philosophy of Religion* 63 (2008) 71–86.

Ferngren, Gary B. *Science and Religion: A Historical Introduction*. Baltimore: Johns Hopkins University Press, 2002.

Ferré, Frederick. "Mapping the Logic of Models in Science and Theology." *The Christian Scholar* 14 (1963) 9–39.

Flew, Anthony, editor. *New Essays in Philosophical Theology*. London: SCM, 1961.

Fodor, Jerry. "Is Science Biologically Possible?" In *Naturalism Defeated: Essays on Plantinga's Evolutionary Argument against Naturalism*, 30–42. Ithaca, NY: Cornell University Press, 2002.

Giberson, Karl. *Oracles of Science: Celebrity Scientists versus God and Religion*. Oxford: Oxford University Press, 2006.

Giere, Ronald N. "How Models Are Used to Represent Reality." *Philosophy of Science* 71 (2004) 742–52.

Green, Joel B., Stuart L. Palmer, and Kevin Corcoran. *In Search of the Soul: Four Views of the Mind-Body Problem*. Downers Grove, IL: InterVarsity, 2005.

Gregerson, Niels Henrik. "Three Varieties of Panentheism." In *In Whom We Live and Move and Have Our Being: Panentheistic Reflections on God's Presence in a Scientific World*, edited by Philip Clayton and A. R. Peacocke, 19–35. Grand Rapids: Eerdmans, 2004.

Haack, Susan. "Six Signs of Scientism." *Logos and Episteme* 3.1 (2012). Online: http://www.logos-and-episteme.proiectsbc.ro/.

Hasker, William. *The Emergent Self*. Ithaca, NY: Cornell University Press, 1999.

Hawking, Stephen. *A Brief History of Time*. New York: Bantam, 2010.

———. *The Grand Design*. New York: Bantam, 2010.

Hesse, Mary B. *Models and Analogies in Science*. South Bend, IN: University of Notre Dame Press, 1966.

Hick, John, editor. *Classical and Contemporary Readings in the Philosophy of Religion*. 2nd ed. Englewood Cliff, NJ: Prentice-Hall, 1970.

Johnston, Mark. *Saving God: Religion after Idolatry*. Princeton: Princeton University Press, 2009.

Jones, J. R. "Love as Perception of Meaning." In *Religion and Understanding*, edited by D. Z. Phillips, 141–54. Oxford: Blackwell, 1967.

Kazdin, Alan. "Evidence-Based Treatment and Practice: New Opportunities to Bridge Clinical Research and Practice, Enhance the Knowledge Base, and Improve Patient Care." *American Psychologist*, 63.3 (2008) 146–59.

Keeley, Brian L. *Paul Churchland*. Contemporary Philosophy in Focus. Cambridge: Cambridge University Press, 2006.

Kim, Jaegwon. "Being Realist about Emergence." In *The Re-Emergence of Emergence: The Emergentist Hypothesis from Science to Religion*, edited by Philip Clayton and Paul Davies, 189–202. Oxford: Oxford University Press, 2006.

———. *Physicalism, or Something Near Enough*. Princeton Monographs in Philosophy. Princeton, NJ: Princeton University Press, 2005.

Klemke, E. D. *The Meaning of Life*. New York: Oxford University Press, 1981.

Kornblith, Hilary. *Naturalizing Epistemology*. 2nd ed. Boston: MIT, 1994.

Lindbeck, George, *The Nature of Doctrine: Religion and Theology in a Postliberal Age*. Philadelphia: Westminster John Knox, 1984.

Liston, Dan, et al. "NCLB and Scientifically-Based Research: Opportunities Lost and Found." *Journal of Teacher Education* 58.2 (2007) 99–107

Loewer, Barry. "Review of *Mind in a Physical World: An Essay on the Mind-Body Problem and Mental Causation* by Jaegwon Kim." *The Journal of Philosophy* 98.6 (2001) 315–24.

Malcolm, Norman. *Wittgenstein: A Religious Point of View?* New York: Routledge, 1997.

McClintock, Robert. "Educational Research." No page numbers. *Teachers College Record*, March (2007). Online: http://www.tcrecord.org.

McFague, Sallie. *Metaphorical Theology: Models of God in Religious Language*. Philadelphia: Fortress, 1982.

McGrath, Alister E. *Science and Religion: An Introduction*. Oxford: Blackwell, 1999.

Moore, Andrew. *Realism and Christian Faith: God, Grammar, and Meaning*. Cambridge: Cambridge University Press, 2003.

Moore, Gareth. *Believing in God: A Philosophical Essay*. Edinburgh: T. & T. Clark, 1988.

Moreland, J. P. *Consciousness and the Existence of God: A Theistic Argument*. New York: Routledge, 2008.

Newton, Isaac. *The Principia*. Translated by Andrew Motte. 1729. Reprint. Great Mind Series. Amherst, NY: Prometheus, 1995.

No Child Left Behind (NCLB). No page numbers. http://www2.ed.gov/policy/elsec/ leg/esea02/index.html.

Nuland, Sherwin B. *How We Die: Reflections on Life's Final Chapter*. New York: Vintage, 1995.

Olson, Richard G. *Science Deified & Science Defied: The Historical Significance of Science in Western Culture.* Vol. 2. Berkeley: University of California Press, 1995.

Otto, Rudolf. *The Idea of the Holy: An Inquiry into the Non-Rational Factor in the Idea of the Divine and Its Relation to the Rational.* 2nd ed. Oxford: Oxford University Press, 1950.

Paley, William. *Natural Theology: Or, Evidences of the Existence and Attributes of the Deity, Collected from the Appearances of Nature.* In *Philosophy: The Quest for Truth,* 6th ed., edited by Louis Pojman, 83–85. Oxford: Oxford University Press, 2006.

Pascal, Blaise. *Pensées.* Translated by Roger Ariew. Indianapolis, IN.: Hackett, 2005.

Pattison, George. *The Philosophy of Kierkegaard.* Continental European Philosophy. Montreal: Mcgill-Queen's University Press, 2005.

Peacocke, Arthur. *All That Is: A Naturalistic Faith for the 21st Century.* Minneapolis, MN: Fortress, 2007.

———. "Articulating God's Presence In and To the World Unveiled by the Sciences." In *In Whom We Live and Move and Have Our Being: Panentheistic Reflections on God's Presence in a Scientific World,* edited by Philip Clayton and A. R. Peacocke, 137–55. Grand Rapids: Eerdmans, 2004.

———. *Paths from Science towards God: The End of All Our Exploring.* Oxford: OneWorld, 2001

———. *Theology for a Scientific Age: Being and Becoming—Natural, Divine and Human.* Minneapolis, MN: Augsburg Fortress, 1993.

Peirce, C. S. *The Essential Peirce: Selected Philosophical Writings, Volume 2 (1893–1913).* Bloomington, IN: Indiana University Press, 1998.

Pennock, Robert T. *Intelligent Design Creationism and Its Critics: Philosophical, Theological, and Scientific Perspectives.* Cambridge: MIT, 2001.

Phillips, D. Z. *Death and Immortality.* London: Macmillan, 1970.

———. *Faith and Philosophical Enquiry.* New York: Schocken, 1970.

———. "Minds, Persons, and the Unthinkable." In *Minds and Persons,* edited by Anthony O'Hear, 49–66. Cambridge: Cambridge University Press, 2003.

———. *The Problem of Evil and The Problem of God.* Minneapolis, MN: Fortress, 2005.

———. *Recovering Religious Concepts: Closing Epistemic Divides.* London: Macmillan, 2000.

———. *Religion Without Explanation,* Oxford: Blackwell, 1976.

———. *Wittgenstein and Religion.* New York: Saint Martin's, 1993.

Placher, William C. *Readings in the History of Christian Theology, from the Reformation to the Present.* Vol. 2. Philadelphia: Westminster, 1988.

Plantinga, Alvin, and Daniel C. Dennett. *Science and Religion: Are They Compatible?* Oxford: Oxford University Press, 2010.

Pojman, Louis. *Philosophy: The Quest for Truth.* 6th ed. Oxford: Oxford University Press, 2006.

Polkinghorne, John. *Science and Theology: An Introduction.* Minneapolis, MN: Augsburg Fortress, 1998.

Quine, W. V. *Ontological Relativity, and Other Essays.* New York: Columbia University Press, 1969.

———. "On the Reasons for Indeterminacy of Translation." *Journal of Philosophy* 67 (1970) 178–83.

———. *Pursuit of Truth.* Cambridge: Harvard University Press, 1992.

Ramsey, Ian. *Models and Mystery.* Oxford: Oxford University Press, 1964.

Ratzsch, Del. *Science and Its Limits*. Downers Grove, IL: InterVarsity, 2000.

Rhees, Rush. *Without Answers*. London: Routledge, 1969.

Rorty, Richard. *Objectivity, Relativism, and Truth*. Cambridge: Cambridge University Press, 1991.

Russell, Bertrand. *Introduction to Mathematical Philosophy*. New York: Macmillan, 1919.

Schleiermacher, Friedrich. *The Christian Faith*. Translated and edited by H. R. Mackintosh and J. S. Stewart. 1928. Reprint. London: T. & T. Clark, 1999.

Savellos, Elias E., and Ümit D. Yalçin. *Supervenience: New Essays*. Cambridge: Cambridge University Press, 1995.

Shostak, Stanley. *The Evolution of Death: Why We Are Living Longer*. Albany, NY: SUNY, 2006.

Smedes, Taede A. *Chaos, Complexity, and God: Divine Action and Scientism*. Leuven: Peeters, 2004.

Snow, C. P. *The Two Cultures*. Cambridge: Cambridge University Press, 1993.

Sober, Elliott. *Evidence and Evolution: The Logic Behind the Science*. Cambridge: Cambridge University Press, 2008.

Stenger, Victor J. "Physics, Cosmology and the New Creationism." University of Colorado. Online: *www.colorado.edu/philosophy/vstenger/RelSci/CosmicCreationism.pdf*.

Strandberg, Hugo. *The Possibility of Discussion: Relativism, Truth, and Criticism of Religious Beliefs*. Aldershot, UK: Ashgate, 2007.

Tanenbaum, Sandra J. "Evidence-Based Practice as Mental Health Policy: Three Controversies and a Caveat." *Health Affairs* 24.1 (2005). Online: http://content .healthaffairs.org/ cgi/content/full/24/1/163.

Thurmon, Robert. *Infinite Life: Awakening to Bliss Within*. New York: Riverhead, 2004.

Tillich, Paul. *The Courage to Be*. New Haven, CT: Yale University Press, 1952.

———. *Systematic Theology*, vol. 1. Chicago: University of Chicago Press, 1951.

Tilghman, Benjamin R. *An Introduction to the Philosophy of Religion*. Introducing Philosophy. Oxford: Blackwell, 1994.

Tolstoy, Leo. *The Death of Ivan Ilyich and Other Stories*. Translated by Rosemary Edmonds. New York: Penguin, 1960.

———. *My Confessions*. In *The Meaning of Life*, edited by E. D. Klemke, 9–19. Oxford: Oxford University Press, 1981.

Twain, Mark. *Life on the Mississippi*. New York: Harper, 1901.

Van Fraassen, Bas C. *The Empirical Stance*. New Haven, CT: Yale University Press, 2002.

Van Inwagen, Peter. *Metaphysics*. Boulder, CO: Westview, 1993.

Wallace, David Foster. "Joseph Frank's Dostoevsky." In *Consider the Lobster*, 255–74. New York: Little and Brown, 2005.

Ward, Keith. *God, a Guide for the Perplexed*. Oxford: Oneworld, 2002.

Weil, Simone. *Gravity and Grace*. Lincoln, NE: Bison, 1997.

———. *Waiting for God*. Translated by Arthur Wills. Lincoln, NE: Bison, 1997.

Weinberg, Steven. *The First Three Minutes: A Modern View of the Origin of the Universe*. New York: Basic, 1977.

Wisdom, John. "Gods." In *Classical and Contemporary Readings in the Philosophy of Religion*, 2nd ed., edited by John Hick, 429–44. Englewood Cliffs, NJ. Prentice-Hall, 1970.

Wittgenstein, Ludwig. *The Blue and Brown Books*. 2nd ed. Oxford: Blackwell, 1969.

———. *Culture and Value*. Edited by G. H. von Wright. Chicago: University of Chicago Press, 1980.

————. *Lectures and Conversations on Aesthetics, Psychology, and Religious Belief.* Edited by Cyril Barrett. Oxford: Blackwell, 1966.

————. *Philosophical Investigations.* Translated by G. E. M. Anscombe. Oxford: Blackwell, 1953.

————. *Philosophical Occasions, 1912–1951.* Edited by James Carl Klagge and Alfred Nordmann. Indianapolis, IN: Hackett, 1993.

————. *Tractatus Logico-Philosophicus.* Translated by C. K. Ogden. Mineola, NY: Dover, 1999.

Worthing, Mark William. *God, Creation, and Contemporary Physics* Minneapolis, MN: Fortress, 1996.

Index